Praise for The Passion Plan at Work

"Richard Chang is the first to both identify passion as the root force behind performance excellence and to provide a clear roadmap for how to achieve it. His recommendations for developing a passion-driven organizational purpose and strategic plan make this a value-added read for leaders of startups and Fortune 500s alike."

—P. George Benson, Dean, Terry College of Business, University of Georgia

"I treasure every opportunity to learn from Richard Chang. *The Passion Plan at Work* offers wisdom for every leader in every organization. Richard's step-by-step plan and practical examples provide an approach that guarantees success. Good job, Richard!"

—Elaine Biech, author of *The Business of Consulting*

"In a time of record employment, when talented people can day-trade their careers, the number one issue for businesses is maintaining a committed, energized workforce. Whether we are executives, managers, team leaders, or just trying to manage our own work life, we all struggle with how to approach this task. Chang's book hits the challenge head-on and delivers us a way to think and act at the core of what makes organizations great."

—John Cone, Vice President, Dell Learning, Dell Computer Corporation

"Before reading *The Passion Plan at Work* it was difficult to believe that a book could explain how passion drives performance in any organization. Dr. Chang clearly describes the steps needed to embrace a true 'heart-to-heart' relationship in your organization."

—Dale Crownover, President and CEO of Texas Nameplate Company, Winner of the 1998 Malcolm Baldrige National Quality Award

"Chang goes to the 'head' of the class by getting to the 'heart' of what drives organizations. He demonstrates how passion provides the vital link between purpose and profit."

—Len Farano, Quality Management Director, Citigroup

"I have long held the view that the organizations that sustain success over the long term nurture a careful blending of passion and process. Richard Chang offers sage advice as to how to accomplish this in his book *The Passion Plan at Work*."

—Gary Floss, Vice President, Corporate Quality, Medtronic, Inc.

"*The Passion Plan at Work* brings timely attention to what is perhaps the largest untapped source of energy and productivity in the marketplace: raw passion. This important book starts with the heart and guides us in building a powerful emotional relationship with our work, one that will sustain us in good times and bad."

—Stephen C. Lundin, coauthor of *FISH! A Remarkable Way to Boost Morale and Improve Results*

"In *The Passion Plan at Work*, Dr. Chang has developed a critical tool for leaders to assist them in creating synergy through organizational passion to allow an organization to achieve its greatest potential."

—Brenda K. Kuhn, Vice President, White Memorial Medical Center

"Harnessing the passion of your employees will ensure organizational success and competitiveness. Richard Chang's new book, *The Passion Plan at Work*, gives senior executives a practical blueprint to release the limitless energy in employees deeply committed to your mission."

—Louise Liang, M.D., President, Group Health Permanente; Medical Director, Group Health Cooperative

"Far too often, organizations and their strategies are just too logical . . . appealing to the head but completely missing the energy and passion that come from the heart. *The Passion Plan at Work* is a must-read for anyone who wants to build their organization by capturing the emotional drive that burns in all of us."

—Robert J. Maple, Senior Vice President, Human
Resources, Dade Behring Inc.

"Organizations that can tap the passion of a diverse workforce will win the biggest challenge of the 21st century, the competition for talent. In *The Passion Plan at Work*, Richard Chang shows you why and tells you how."

— Frederick A. Miller, President and CEO, The Kaleel
Jamison Consulting Group, Inc.

"Richard takes you to the core of your organization, into the hearts of your people, and in the process, reveals a practical strategy for success in the 21st century."

—Donnee Ramelli, President, General Motors
University

"This is one terrific book—not only to read it, but to live by it. *The Passion Plan at Work* makes passion a way of life in organizations; it provides cutting-edge thinking and substantive prescriptions to stimulate threshold passion and leverage intellectual assets in 'passion-seeking' environments. *The Passion Plan* is yet another manifestation of Dr. Chang's staggering influences on the performances and productivity of corporate America."

—A. Tarzi, Senior National Human Resources Manager,
American Suzuki Motor Corporation

"Enormous energy and capacity exist inside most people, but most organizations unwittingly bottle it up. *The Passion Plan* provides a practical guide to uncork the bottle and release this pent-up force."

—Jack Zenger, Vice Chairman, Provant, Inc.

"*The Passion Plan at Work* reminds all of us who have had a passion in our lives of the true power that can accompany it. The potential for businesses is mind-boggling."

—Kimberly Janson, Director, Organizational
Effectiveness and Workforce Diversity, Hasbro, Inc.

"*The Passion Plan at Work* links process and passion to align employee commitment, capability, and satisfaction with organizational performance and success. In demonstrating how passion is critical to achieving and sustaining organizational goals and objectives, Richard Chang fundamentally alters how we consider and implement organizational change. A passionate read for anyone wrestling with today's personal and organizational performance challenges."

—Michael G. Hansen, Senior Vice President,
Veridian Corporation

The Passion Plan at Work

The Passion Plan at Work

Building a Passion-Driven Organization

Richard Chang

JOSSEY-BASS
A Wiley Company
San Francisco

Jossey-Bass books and products are available through most bookstores. To contact
Jossey-Bass directly, call (888) 378-2537, fax to (800) 605-2665, or visit our website at
www.josseybass.com.

Substantial discounts on bulk quantities of Jossey-Bass books are available to
corporations, professional associations, and other organizations. For details and
discount information, contact the special sales department at Jossey-Bass.

Printed in the United States of America.

Interior design by Paula Goldstein.

Library of Congress Cataloging-in-Publication Data
Chang, Richard Y.
    The passion plan at work : building a passion-driven organization /
by Richard Chang.
        p.   cm.
Includes bibliographical references and index.
    ISBN 0-7879-5255-9
    1. Organizational effectiveness. 2. Leadership. I. Title.
    HD58.9.C482 2001
    658—dc21   00-011966

FIRST EDITION
HB Printing   10 9 8 7 6 5 4 3 2 1

To my parents, William and Catherine,
my sister and brother-in-law, Sophia and C.T.,
and niece Kasen
for continuing to support me in my passion pursuits.
Thank you for your encouragement, love,
and support along the journey.

To the owners, executives, managers, and employees
in passion-driven organizations
who continue to keep the passion alive and live it every day.

To the past and current associates
at Richard Chang Associates, Inc.,
who have helped me keep my passion alive
and contributed your personal passion
to our organization's success.

Contents

Chapter 4

Chapter 5

Chapter 6

Chapter 7

Chapter 8

Chapter 9

Chapter 10

The Author

Richard Chang has been driven by his passion for personal and organizational excellence all his life. In his youth, he mastered three musical instruments and excelled at a variety of competitive sports—including roller skating, tennis, swimming, water polo, volleyball, and bowling. As a freshman at UCLA, he won the National Collegiate Singles Championship in bowling, was named amateur bowler of the year for Southern California, and later bowled on the professional tour.

Chang is CEO of Richard Chang Associates, Inc., a performance improvement consulting, training, and publishing firm headquartered in Irvine, California. He is internationally recognized for his strategic planning, performance measurement, quality improvement, organization development, product realization, change management, customer service, and human resource development expertise. As an internal business practitioner, he held management and senior leadership positions in four organizations. He has served as an external consultant to a wide variety of domestic and international organizations—including Toshiba, Citibank, McDonald's, Marriott, Universal Studios, Fidelity Investments, Black & Decker, Chase Manhattan, Nortel Networks, Suzuki, Disneyland, Air New Zealand, Levi Strauss, Brazosport Independent School District, Booz-Allen & Hamilton, and Nabisco.

Chang is the author or coauthor of more than twenty books on business and personal development and is the award-winning author of more than twelve training videotapes, including *The Passion Plan—Putting Your Passion to Work*. His works have been published in over ten different languages internationally.

He served as the 1999 chair of the board for the American Society for Training and Development and has been a judge for the prestigious Malcolm Baldrige National Quality Award in the United States. Chang has a Ph.D. in industrial and organizational psychology and has been cited in *Outstanding Young Men of America, Who's Who in Leading American Executives,* and *International Who's Who in Quality.*

In addition to his business experience, Chang has also been a therapist in private practice and community-clinic settings and has served as adjunct faculty of several universities and community colleges. As a top-rated and engaging keynote speaker, he addresses a wide range of audiences at conferences and corporate events around the world.

foreword

When I started Federal Express back in 1973, we had a small group of employees, an even smaller fleet of aircraft, and an idea. I knew that air express delivery could revolutionize the shipping industry and that our new company could be the one to do it. I was confident, but more important, I was passionate about it. Twenty-seven years later this passion still burns strong. In fact, it is the heart of the entire FedEx Corporation. As market conditions and strategies have changed—and as our business has grown—our passion has remained constant. It's a passion to deliver far more than packages. It's a passion to deliver success for every customer. That passionate spirit of FedEx has set us apart from our competitors and fueled our success in a way nothing else could.

In this book, Richard Chang shows how organizations in any field can use passion to succeed. After spending the last twenty-five years building his own passion-based business and advising hundreds of others, he understands that today passion is a necessity for business success. He has distilled years of experience into a seven-step plan that any organization can use to improve and succeed.

The lessons do not require any complicated analyses or calculations. Instead, Richard Chang shows you how to get to the heart of your business. He helps you identify the forces that stir emotion in your organization and shows you how to use that emotion as the platform for future successes. Regardless of where an organization currently falls on the Passion Scale, it can be reinvigorated around passion.

Successful leaders of the future will have to tap into the tremendous potential passion offers them. In fact, despite the advances in both physical networks and information networks that drive the high-tech and high-speed New Economy, successful leaders must invest in a third and vital network—a passionate people network that sparks the ideas and innovation for lasting success.

At FedEx we learned these lessons early and have never relented in the pursuit of our core passions. We focus on our people, our service, and our profits. As FedEx employees will attest, work becomes fun and rewarding when it draws on individual passions. Our first-line leaders will concur that meeting and exceeding our goals becomes easier and, I'm sure, more exciting when everyone is united by common passions.

I'm very pleased that Richard Chang has taken the time to share his expertise on passion by writing this book. Contrary to what some might think, there is no secret weapon or magic solution that successful organizations guard jealously. Passion is a great advantage, and those who have it are generally eager to share it and have others benefit as a result. As you'll learn in the pages that follow, passion can build better companies, create better products and services, and improve the lives of all those it touches—customers, employees, partners, and communities.

It is my hope that you can use this book to strengthen your organization. The future will be shaped by those organizations and individuals who are aware of their passions and have the courage to pursue them. At FedEx, we plan on being at the forefront of such companies. Good luck in your quest to put passion in your organization.

Frederick W. Smith
Chairman and CEO
FedEx Corporation
November 2000

Preface

My book *The Passion Plan: A Step-by-Step Guide to Discovering, Developing, and Living Your Passion* was published in late 1999. I was inspired to write it because of my own experiences with living my passion. In my life I have learned that passion can be a tremendous source of personal enrichment and success, but that, sadly, most people are too afraid or confused to embrace it. In *The Passion Plan* I showed individuals how to identify their passions and use them to build more productive and fulfilling lives, to realize what I call "Profit with a capital P."

"Profit with a capital P" is any outcome we seek as a result of our actions. It can take any number of forms: career, family, financial, spiritual, and so on. The capital letter in *Profit* signifies that the intended rewards are not just of abundance but also of enrichment. They have meaning. They don't merely add, they improve.

When I wrote *The Passion Plan*, I knew this book would follow. After approximately twenty-five years in the business management, personal development, and consulting field, I have learned that the organizational definition of Profit is changing, and that the criteria for success no longer revolve strictly around profit and loss statements. As a result many organizations, both young and old, are struggling to leave the old era but do not know how to enter the new one. To these companies, corporations, foundations, and groups, I offer these words: Those organizations that truly excel, that realize their Profit, are predicated on passion. By proudly proclaiming their passions and pursuing them with gusto, these organizations accomplish things their competitors only dream of. They attract and retain superior employees, wow customers with superior products and services, and have fun doing what they do. This is true whether they are "built to last" or—as a recent *Fast Company* cover proclaimed— "built to flip" (be sold).

I have written this second Passion Plan book because I know that for every individual seeking passion, there is an organization hoping to do the same. Although many good companies enjoy financial successes based on solid products or reliable services, they often lack the emotion and vitality that can take them to a higher level. They have not discovered the keys to invigorating their employees and supercharging their operations. They have not yet reached their full potential or claimed the advantages that passion offers. Clearly, building a passion-driven organization is an important "business strategy," not just a nice thing to do.

The seven-step plan presented in this book gives organizations a way to claim passion as their own and to turn good companies into great ones. To illustrate how each step works and the different ways of approaching it, I interviewed and researched the following twelve superior organizations for support and reference throughout the book: Ben & Jerry's

Homemade, Disney Institute, Gateway, GTE Directories, Brazosport Independent School District, Wainwright Industries, Clarke American, McLeodUSA, PSS/World Medical, EarthLink, MindSpring, and Southwest Airlines. I selected these organizations based on their diversity, their accomplishments, and, most important, their dedication to passion. They have won industry awards and critical acclaim, earned financial profits and professional respect, and gained the loyalty of customers and associates by acknowledging their passions and pursuing them without apology.

Some of these organizations—and the business conditions under which they operate—have changed since the research and data-gathering phase of writing this book. For example, Ben & Jerry's has recently been acquired. GTE Corporation has since merged with Bell Atlantic to form Verizon Communications. Some of the individuals interviewed for their respective organizations have made personal career changes, and business plans may have evolved due to changing market conditions. Nonetheless, all the information and examples referenced in the book are valid examples of how passion has been instilled and leveraged in the organizations described.

This book possesses the greatest potential for change in the hands of leaders. Owners, CEOs, and senior managers have the authority and means necessary to introduce lasting and significant change within the organization. After all, doing so requires their vision, commitment, and ongoing leadership. But it can also be powerful when used by associates to implement change from the bottom up. Each and every person involved in an organization has the potential to strengthen and improve performance. And when passion is involved the possibility that the changes will spread increases exponentially.

It is my fervent hope that no matter what position you hold in your organization, you will find *The Passion Plan at Work* useful. I hope that it will inspire you to cultivate passion within your organization and your work and to share it with others—other employees, other leaders, other colleagues, other organizations—so that one day we may all reap its rewards.

As you progress through the book, I encourage you to make notes and complete the worksheets at the end of the chapters—gradually creating your own Passion Plan within your organization. I'm anxious to hear about your personal experiences applying the principles described in *The Passion Plan at Work*. Please visit **www.thepassionplan.com** to share your personal and organizational stories about how you've been "living the Passion Plan" and to review examples from other readers, or e-mail your stories to **thepassionplan@rca4results.com.**

Read on. I extend you this challenge: Let passion in!

Wishing you success,
Richard Chang
Irvine, California
November 2000

Acknowledgments

When I decided to write this follow-on book to *The Passion Plan: A Step-by-Step Guide to Discovering, Developing, and Living Your Passion*, I knew that the experience would be quite different from the experiences I had when writing the first book in the series. This book needed to move from the focus on individuals to the focus on organizations and their ability to inspire and lead a number of individuals, each with varying passions, to collectively embrace a common passion.

It needed to be inspirational, motivational, and genuine in conveying the importance of discovering and living organizational passion, but not at the expense of the passions of individuals in the organizations. And finally, it needed to be realistic and practical, providing examples of how to actually turn the subjective emotion or feeling of passion into an objective and manageable plan of action for an organization.

Overall, thanks to my professional colleagues, friends, and acquaintances that have helped me to shape and live my passions over the years as our paths have crossed. You have all been a part of my own Passion Plan.

Special thanks go to the following:

- Anne Andrus, my talented writer and researcher, for helping me turn a lifetime of experiences and ideas into a meaningful written message. Your personal energy and passion for the subject matter were indispensable contributors to the completion of the manuscript.
- The team of impassioned associates at Richard Chang Associates, Inc., for encouraging and supporting me throughout the book development process. In particular, I'd like to extend my special thanks to Jill Hennigan, Denise Jeffrey, Rich Baisner, Donna Campbell, and Melissa Zirretta, who provided a variety of "extra" support in preparing drafts, reviewing content, documenting information, designing graphics, and supporting a wide variety of marketing and book completion logistics.
- The team of talented professionals at Jossey-Bass, Inc., for providing a variety of editing, marketing, and production support that helped to bring this book to reality. In particular, I'd like to extend my special thanks to Susan Williams, my talented editor, for being so collaborative, supportive, and encouraging throughout the manuscript development process; to Katie Crouch, Paula Goldstein, and Mary Garrett, for helping me keep on track with the variety of deliverables needed to complete the design and production of the book; and to the sales, publicity, and marketing team for your efforts in getting this book into the hands of impassioned readers around the world.
- My extended family of relatives, close friends, business colleagues, and clients, for being supportive, challenging,

and believing in me along the way and as I continue to live my passions every day.

- And finally, I'd like to acknowledge you—the reader of this book—for having the curiosity, interest, and courage to get in touch with your true passions and take the necessary actions in your organization to live them on the job. I wish you the best in living your personal Passion Plan at Work.

The
Passion Plan
at Work

Passionism...

"Passion is not a privilege of the fortunate few; it is a right and competitive advantage that all oranizations can leverage."

CHAPTER 1

Why Passion Works in Organizations

A Timeless Source for Timely Change

We are minor in everything but our passions.
—Elizabeth Bowen

In 1993, Sky Dayton was twenty-two years old. An avid snowboarder with a warm smile, at first glance he probably seemed like most guys his age: emerging into adulthood uncertain of where he was headed. Those who knew him well, however, understood that the similarities between Sky and his peers ended with this appearance. Underneath the youthful countenance dwelled a seasoned entrepreneur, skilled and driven beyond his years. And not just any entrepreneur, but one poised to claim a prominent place in the annals of twentieth-century technology.

At nineteen, Sky opened a successful coffeehouse in West Hollywood, and at twenty-one he co-founded a respected graphics design firm. He was passionate about building his own businesses and saw no limits to his possibilities.

One night as he was driving home from the coffeehouse he was struck by an idea. After spending more than eighty hours trying to get connected to the then fledgling Internet, he realized that there had to be an easier way. And why shouldn't he be the one to come up with it? Computers had always captivated him. And his enthusiasm had grown when he saw their potential as a tool of communication. The Internet promised to be the next mass medium and he was excited about finding a way to bring it to people.

Once the idea had taken root, Sky was unstoppable. He was filled with an energy that propelled him past any obstacles that stood in his way. Within a few months he had raised enough money to set up a six-hundred-square-foot office powered by ten modems. Within a few years, his little venture—called EarthLink Network—had grown into the world's second-largest Internet Service Provider, or ISP, serving over one million users and blazing a trail as an innovator in the world of Web access.

While Sky was working his magic on the West Coast, Charles Brewer was finding similar success back east. A graduate of Stanford Business School, Charles had reached the level of CEO at an Atlanta technology firm. He was successful but unhappy. After viewing the business world from the inside as an employee and from the outside as a consumer, he had come to a startling realization. There was something fundamentally wrong with corporate America. Customers were frustrated and employees were stifled by organizations that didn't care about them or their needs.

Committed to finding a better way, Charles walked away from his chief executive position and took some time to develop a set of Core Values and Beliefs that would serve as the foundation for his ideal company. He didn't know what the company would do, what product or service it would provide, but that didn't really matter. What did matter was that the organization would be different. It would be guided by higher principles and devoted to improving the lives of its customers and employees.

With his Core Values and Beliefs defined, Charles was ready to get started. The inspiration for his company came when, like Sky, he tried to get connected to the Internet. Exasperated by the difficulty of his experience, he assembled a hodgepodge of equipment and a group of employees dedicated to his ideals and committed to making the average person's Internet experience enjoyable.

Five years later MindSpring Enterprises had grown to employ two thousand people and serve over a million users. It was rated number one in customer satisfaction by J. D. Power and Associates (EarthLink was number two) and was lauded in business circles for its policies and practices.

Passion Is the Key to Twenty-First-Century Success

At the dawn of the new century, there were over five thousand ISPs in this country, but EarthLink and MindSpring were in the top five. They rose to this level with far fewer resources and much less power than industry behemoths such as AT&T and Microsoft. What distinguished them from the thousands of others? Luck? Maybe. Strategy? Partially. Skill? Definitely. But many of their competitors shared similar expertise. What truly set them apart and enabled them to succeed in a field where so many struggle? I believe the answer is simple: passion.

Sky Dayton was brimming with it. He couldn't sleep at night, he was so motivated by his desire to bring the Internet to the masses. He was driven by his passion to help people communicate and he infused EarthLink with that same spirit. In the early days he hired people who shared his passion and were excited about the organization's mission. As he told me recently, "It was absolutely critical that everyone have a passion for the Internet and what we were doing." As the organization has grown, customers and employees alike have been drawn to the company not only because of the level of service it provides, but because they sense its commitment, intensity, and enthusiasm.

Charles Brewer's passion was different from Sky's, but it led him in a similar direction. He was committed first and foremost to the creation of a better organization, one that treated its customers well and gave its employees the freedom and inspiration to do great work. Unlike EarthLink, Mind-Spring hired its employees based not on their passion for the Internet but largely for their enthusiasm for the organization's Core Values and Beliefs, which included honesty, respect, and frugality. Customers were attracted to these same values. Most remained fiercely loyal to the company, and, like EarthLink, MindSpring boasted extraordinary customer retention rates. In an industry where the average *churn rate* (the percentage of customers discontinuing service each month) is 6–8 percent, MindSpring traditionally lost only 3–3.5 percent.

EarthLink and MindSpring merged in early 2000. Though historically the organizations were motivated by different passions, the heads of both organizations felt that their shared dedication to customers would enable them to prevail in the marketplace. The new organization, known as Earth-

Link, Inc., adopted the MindSpring Core Values and Beliefs and has focused on establishing itself as the leading ISP in the world. Though both acknowledge that the transition presents challenges, they also feel that their underlying passions will enable them to overcome them. By combining EarthLink's passion for the Internet with MindSpring's passion for organizational excellence, the new company stands poised to set the Internet world on fire.

Both EarthLink and MindSpring demonstrate the most practical and enduring lesson I have learned over twenty-five years of helping to improve individual and organizational performance: *passion is the single most powerful competitive advantage an organization can claim in building its success.* Many organizations possess the same technology, resources, equipment, and expertise in their employees, but it is the organization that runs on passion that prevails. The passion-driven organization inspires its employees, invigorates its customers, and reaps the benefits of their shared enthusiasm in its success. And not only does the passion-driven organization win the battle with its competitors, it often achieves its victory with less perceived effort and difficulty than those lacking the same emotion.

Passion in the Organization

In *The Passion Plan,* I defined passion as personal intensity, or the underlying force that fuels our strongest emotions. You may recognize it not by how it's named but rather by what it does. Passion fills you with energy and excitement. It gets you up in the morning and keeps you awake at night. When you experience it, you lose track of time and become absorbed in the task at hand. It uplifts you and inspires you. It heightens your performance and enables you to achieve things you may never have dreamed possible.

Just as we can be guided and inspired by our individual passions, so can organizations be driven and defined by their collective passions. A footwear company may draw its inspiration from a passion for fashion or a burning desire to make people comfortable. A publishing house might be motivated by a love of literature or a dedication to education. Either could be prompted by a commitment to creating a superior organization or being the best in its field.

No matter what type of business, passion can and should play a vital role. The irony is that often it does not. It might seem obvious that a shoe manufacturer should love shoes or that a publisher should be crazy about books, but many times this is simply not the case. Historically businesses have been created to fill a need in the market and deliver a profit to their shareholders. They have been judged by the numbers they deliver and not by the spirit they possess.

Times are changing, and success is no longer as simple as a solid bottom line. While profits are still critical to an organization's survival, the ways to achieve them are not so straightforward. Consumers are more savvy and face more options in the marketplace. They expect superior quality and friendly service. Employees find their skills in great demand and require more from the companies that employ them. They expect employers to value them, pay them well, and provide meaning in their work. Communities have also raised the bar on expectations. They expect the businesses that line their streets to contribute time, effort, and money to their improvement.

Fulfilling these expectations while turning a profit has become a formidable task indeed. Even if an organization finds ways to please each group, it must then be quick enough to respond to changes in technology and smart enough to anticipate new directions in the marketplace. "You snooze, you lose" has become the rule of the day. Those companies that are too slow or too cautious to adapt do not survive. Those that try to redefine themselves to keep up often lose focus and flounder in uncertainty.

Consultants and business leaders worldwide have attempted to address these challenges and create new definitions of organizational excellence, to delineate the characteristics that will ensure business success in the new millennium. Among the most notable systems for promoting success are Total Quality Management (TQM), performance measurement scorecards, and benchmarking. I will not explain them in detail, other than to highlight that each focuses on measurement as a means of improving performance. In the right settings in the right organizations, these are highly effective tools. But if something very basic is missing, they are exercises in futility.

Consider this example. A furniture manufacturer in North Carolina has faced diminishing sales over the past five years and is in danger of going out of business. The CEO turns to a consulting firm to analyze the company's weaknesses and suggest solutions to its problems. After months of observation, the consultant arrives at the following conclusions: the products, though high in quality, are outmoded in design; the retailers find the manufacturer difficult to deal with and are abandoning it in favor of competitors; the employees are performing poorly and feel little motivation to improve.

The consultant might then suggest a rigorous program whereby management could set goals and begin to assess the organization's performance. The program might include metrics such as customer satisfaction ratings, employee productivity rankings, and cycle time of the design process. All might prove helpful—if, and only if, there is an underlying passion to support them.

If the designers don't care about customer preferences or view furniture as dull and uninspiring, they might resent or resist changes to their process. If customer service representatives have always been instructed to doubt customers or assume they are wrong, they probably will have a hard time believing they should now treat them with courtesy and respect. If management has traditionally projected an attitude of distrust and control, employees are not likely to suddenly improve their productivity because they are instructed to do so.

What I have found after consulting to countless organizations in continuous improvement and performance measurement techniques is that although many methods alleviate the symptoms that afflict the modern company, few treat the disease that causes them. Those companies that are able not only to succeed but also to excel are built on passion. Though they can encounter problems and face challenges, if passion is present, the solutions are more obvious and effective.

In the case of the furniture manufacturer, its leaders would need to take a good hard look at the business and decide what really mattered. Are they passionate about furniture and willing to take risks to innovate their product line? If so, they could focus primarily on design as a means to improvement. Do they feel a strong desire to be a leader in customer service or employee satisfaction? If so, they could implement customer appreciation or employee education programs as a first step.

Whatever the case, any change they might make would be pointless if it was not grounded in passion. If they were not truly excited about and committed to change, to redefining the organization based on the emotion and vitality of its associates, then any new policies and programs would be hollow attempts at improvement.

You might be surprised by the idea that emotion can be a driving force in business. We often think of business—especially "big business"—as cold and heartless. But consider business instead from the human perspective. A business only exists if there are people to run it and people to purchase its goods and services.

Both employees and customers have feelings that compel them to act the way they do. Employees do not check their personalities at the door and become automatons. Their performance is predicated on their feelings toward their work. Customers do not buy just anything. They make their decisions based on emotional responses to products and the organizations that provide them. Even leaders—from titans of industry to the owners of the mom and pop stores of the world—are subject to emotion. Though they might not always pay attention to their emotions, they have them nonetheless. In some way their feelings have a direct impact on the spirit and success of the organizations they lead.

Getting to the Heart of the Organization

I am by no means the first to recognize the human nature of the organization. In recent years there has been an increasing focus on the need for businesses to focus on those things that most directly impact people and not numbers. Unless you have been living under a rock, you have certainly heard the terms vision, mission, and culture thrown around in business circles. Each theorist assigns different definitions, but collectively they acknowledge a need for emotion in organizations.

People need motivation. They need inspiration. They need something to believe in. They need to feel a sense of belonging, a sense of purpose, and a sense of comfort in everything they do. They do not just crave these things in their homes. They want them in their workplaces, in their shopping malls, and in their online experiences. When organizations address these concerns, they begin to put on a human face.

It would be wrong, however, to assume that businesses can just impose a human element where before there was none. Each organization possesses a heart. There is something deeper than policies and practices that makes it tick, that gives it life. It may beat strong or weak, be heeded or ignored. But it is there.

The success of an organization can depend largely, sometimes entirely, on its respect for the heart.

When I speak to individuals, I explain that there are two types of approaches to living: head-driven and heart-driven. Those who turn primarily to logic and reason for guidance and ignore the prompting of their hearts set themselves up for lives of regret and sadness. They deny the passions that define them and trade enthusiasm and happiness for safety and security.

Those who listen to their hearts and go in directions that

inspire and excite them accomplish their goals and are self-fulfilled. This is not to say that they do not employ reason when making important decisions or planning for their development, only that they give priority to their hearts and the passions they harbor. They understand that the things that move them are also the things that make them. Their passions define who they are and what they can become. As I first described in *The Passion Plan*, I call these people *passioneers*™.

Passioneers achieve something we all are capable of, but many are afraid to try. They make their passions an integral part of their lives and follow them in meaningful ways. In so doing they create their own success. They become productive, excited, and self-fulfilled. They exceed expectations and are fueled by their accomplishments.

The same can be true of organizations. When they pay attention to the forces that truly motivate them, rather than those that seem most logical or those prescribed by outsiders, they tap into a hidden power reserve. They energize their operations and seize the reins of success. They too become passioneers, masters of the art of passioneering.

Passion Review

Passioneers are individuals or organizations that listen to their hearts. They make passion an integral part of their existence and follow it in meaningful ways.

The Benefits of Passion

In an annual letter to shareholders, Sky Dayton and EarthLink CEO Garry Betty made the following claim: "Sure we operate like any of the best fast-growing high-tech enterprises, but in our hearts burns something unique—a passion for what we do that makes every day at EarthLink invigorating and rewarding."

What Sky and Garry emphasize is that an organization predicated on passion is different. It is infused with a special energy and excitement that enables it to achieve more. Earth-Link associates share in the passion and are uplifted and inspired by their involvement. They contribute their best and in so doing reinforce the passion that motivates them to excel.

This may sound like so much lofty language, but I know you have a sense of what I am talking about. Think about the last time you entered a store or an office where you had an unpleasant experience. Perhaps the clerks were hostile or the surroundings depressing. Maybe no one seemed to care whether you got what you needed. Or maybe, and this happens more than you may think, they tried to make it difficult for you to get it.

Now consider the time when you visited a business that impressed you. The employees were friendly, the environment was comfortable, and your experience was actually pleasant. People seemed interested in their work and eager to help you. You probably sensed something different the moment you walked in the door: there was something inviting and engaging about the place. It was filled with an air of enthusiasm, a feeling of excitement.

You felt this way because *passion creates a palpable energy within an organization.* It changes the very nature of its activities. It infuses them with a quality and vitality that otherwise would not be present. The bottom line is that passion transforms the ordinary into the extraordinary.

For those who might believe passion falls into the realm of the touchy-feely, I want to summarize the tangible, often quantifiable, benefits it provides.

1. *Passion provides direction and focus.* When an organization is founded on passion, or discovers and embraces it along the way, that passion defines the direction the business takes. Leadership determines both the purpose and strategy for pursuing it, but although both will change from time to time, passion remains constant. It is the least common denominator to which the organization turns for answers. If a change in the marketplace necessitates a change in practices, then only those practices that reflect the passion will be considered. If a new partner is required, then only those that support the passion will be considered. Regardless of the circumstance, the passion of the organization is the yardstick by which all possibilities are measured and the standard by which all decisions are made.

2. *Passion creates energy.* We all have experienced passion in our lives and recognize the energy rush it provides. When under its influence, we are supercharged. We get so absorbed in our activities that we lose awareness of time and effort. Though we should be exhausted by our efforts, whether mental or physical, we feel energized. What should be difficult is easy. What should take days takes hours. When passion pervades the organization, associates are not only excited about their work, they are also, as Sky Dayton and Garry Betty noted, invigorated by it. On a day-to-day level this extra energy can empower the organization and make the difference between getting the job done and getting it done with distinction.

3.   *Passion fosters creativity.* In a recent study, Harvard Business School professor Teresa M. Amabile argued that the modern organization cannot succeed without "a continuing flow of creative ideas" (Amabile, 1996). Researchers have established that passion can unleash this flow. Passion piques our interest, energy, and attention and heightens our engagement in an activity. With this increased focus and intensity, the barriers to clear and creative thinking are removed. Solutions are forthcoming, alternatives are apparent, and innovation is imminent. When the associates of an organization exercise creativity on both the individual and collective level, the organization gains a unique and valuable self-sufficiency. It is capable of both envisioning its goals and conceiving original ways to achieve them.

4.   *Passion heightens performance.* Increased energy, focus, and creativity all contribute to one end: heightened performance. Passion drives improvements in both the quality and quantity of work performed. Not only do the associates of the organization care about what they are doing, they are constantly motivated to do more and do it better. Their energy and commitment result in increased productivity, efficiency, and stability for the organization. Fueled by the strength of its associates, the organization is capable of greater accomplishment.

5.   *Passion inspires action.* One of the greatest barriers to organizational success is indecisiveness. When leaders are unable to make decisions quickly and confidently, they cripple the organization. It becomes slow and unresponsive to changes in its environment and subsequently ineffective. When possessed by passion, leaders are filled with a can-do spirit that empowers them and the people they lead to take action rather than wallow in indecision. Though the choices

they make and the strategies they employ may not always be the best or even the right ones—this would make them perfect as well as passionate—they are able to move forward with courage and confidence.

6.   *Passion attracts employees and customers.* Perhaps the greatest challenge to the organization today is filling its ranks with first-rate associates. Businesses must compete vigorously to attract qualified employees, who are in increasingly short supply and even greater demand. The passion-driven organization appeals to the superstars of the job market. Motivated and energetic individuals are attracted to environments where their individual passions will be allowed to thrive. They are also eager to commit themselves to the shared passion that defines the organization. In this respect organizations that exude a sense of excitement, that are driven by a strong emotional connection to their enterprise, have a distinct edge over those that do not. Talented employees actually seek them out, not the opposite.

The same is true for customers. A recent study highlighted in the *Wall Street Journal* revealed that customers gravitate toward companies that appeal to them on an emotional level (Alsop, 1999). If they sense passion within an organization, a passion they share or relate to, then they are far more likely to buy that organization's goods or services. It is not the cold fish of the corporate world that succeed with today's consumer. Though there will always be room for them, especially in closed or capital-intensive markets, they will not win any popularity contests. The live wires of the business world are the organizations that win their customers by projecting their energy and enthusiasm into the marketplace.

7.   *Passion builds loyalty.* Passion is not the only way to attract employees and customers. Many are drawn in by the

bottom line—higher wages or lower prices. When the relationship between employer and employee, provider and consumer, is based on money, however, loyalty is not an issue. The relationship ends as soon as a better price or more attractive salary appears. But when relationships are predicated on passion, they are lasting. Both customers and employees remain loyal through the ups and downs of the organization. They are committed emotionally to the success of the business and do not simply walk away when things get difficult. In good times and bad, they act as advocates for the organization, both spreading and sustaining its passion.

8. *Passion unites the organization.* Because passion defines the organization, it is also the force that holds it together. When leaders, employees, and customers share a core passion, they stand on common ground. They may not always agree on details, but they are connected on a deeper level to achieving the organization's objectives. United by passion, employees support leaders and serve customers, leaders represent customers and empower employees, and customers sustain the efforts of the organization.

9. *Passion provides a critical edge.* Passion is uncommon. Though everybody has felt tinges of it, few actually make it an integral part of their lives. Even fewer organizations are able to integrate it successfully into their operations. If passion is alive and at work, the organization that boasts it will stand head and shoulders above its competition. It will find its work enjoyable, its operations easier, and its enthusiasm constant. The passion-driven organization by definition has a distinct edge and with aligned management stands to breeze by its competition.

10. *Passion brings the organization to a higher plane.* Passion-driven organizations are quite simply wonderful places to

work. They are dynamic, engaging, and exciting. They operate on a higher plane than those that lack passion. There is a thrill to their experience. For those involved this thrill manifests as a tangible sense of being engaged in something better, of creating something superior to and more worthwhile than other organizations.

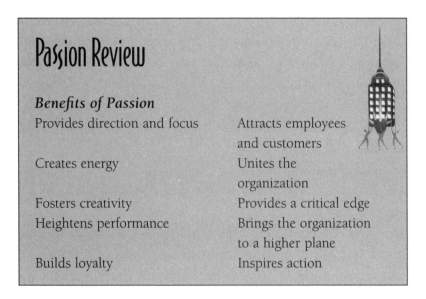

Passion Review

Benefits of Passion

Provides direction and focus	Attracts employees and customers
Creates energy	Unites the organization
Fosters creativity	Provides a critical edge
Heightens performance	Brings the organization to a higher plane
Builds loyalty	Inspires action

How Organizations Lose Sight of Passion

After reviewing this list, you might think that the benefits of passion seem obvious. Of course people are more productive and committed when they are excited. Of course work improves and people have fun when they believe in what they do. Nothing surprising there. What is surprising, however, is that such a valuable resource is often mismanaged and even more often ignored. How is it that passion is not an integral part of most organizations when it provides so much power? Why are so many businesses failing to use it when it is so easy to claim?

There are many reasons organizations lack passion. Some never have it. Some start with it and lose it along the way. Some have it, but fail to recognize it or do not understand how to use it.

I believe that most fall into the last category: at some level there is passion present in the organization, but it does not form the framework. Leadership may feel it, but at the same time not understand how to communicate it to employees. Employees may sense it, but be uncertain or confused as to how to act on it. Customers may detect it in products and services, but may not feel it is consistent or compelling.

Let's consider the case of a hypothetical advertising firm. The organization includes twenty-five people, all of whom are creative and energetic. The three founders met in graduate school and started the business out of a shared passion for promoting ethics and honesty in their industry. Within the first year of business, they were recognized for their creativity with a prestigious award. Very quickly their reputation as an innovator in design grew. Though they still emphasized their commitment to setting a higher ethical standard, they began receiving attention and attracting clients that did not necessarily reflect this desire.

Finding it difficult to turn away business, they began hiring associates and accepting clients based not on their support of their underlying passion, but on their potential to grow the business. They have continued to turn out highly creative work, but often it does not reflect the ideals they were originally committed to. They suffer from high employee turnover as associates hungry for recognition make their creative mark and then move on to other firms who are willing to pay more.

Despite their relative success, the leaders are unhappy with the business they have built. Out of their disappointment, they have considered many options, including selling out to an industry giant of questionable integrity.

Can you see the problem? There may be pockets of passion within the organization, but there is no centralized source. The true passion on which the business was founded has been buried as a matter of pragmatics. People have joined the organization unaware of what it was intended to stand for. Hired for their abilities rather than their passion, some may even be at odds with these ideals. Those who joined in the early days because they shared the founders' passion may be confused by the mixed messages the founders' or leaders' behavior sends. The leaders have failed to articulate their passion to those that work for them, those they serve, and the industry as a whole. The firm has produced work that is inconsistent with its core passion. In fact, it is hard to maintain that a core passion any longer exists.

There are countless businesses out there today that have experienced this same thing. The founders begin their quest with a burning desire and a deep emotional commitment to a principle or idea. They have a passion that guides them. Somewhere along their entrepreneurial journey, however, they lose sight of what it was that originally inspired them. They begin making decisions based on what makes sense rather than what really matters. They compromise their passion again and again until finally it fades away and is forgotten, resulting in frustration, poor performance, and eventually stagnation or failure.

Even if the founders maintain passion in an organization during their tenure, it may disappear after their departure. If they do not effectively spread their passion throughout the organization while still an integral part of it, it will be hard for their successors to maintain it. More important, if they do not ensure that their successors or those responsible for choosing them share this passion, there is little chance their passion will survive them.

Another passion-draining phenomenon that has gripped the business world in the last decade is the desire for unbridled growth. I have witnessed this in many large corporations. Eager to expand, sometimes at any cost, many organizations have attempted to move into areas that do not reflect their core competencies, much less their core passions. Many have swallowed up smaller, thriving organizations only to run them into the ground. This practice defies what I argue to be one of the basic principles of business: *If you don't have a passion for a business, you don't belong in it.*

A manufacturer of film motivated by a passion for the chemistry and technology behind film and photo processing does not necessarily belong in the camera industry. An airline dedicated to safety and convenience may not have the requisite passion to move into the travel agency business. A fast food chain predicated on its founder's love of hamburgers cannot assume its enthusiasm for beef will carry over into the pizza parlor business.

In each of these cases there are connections between the potential partners, and a merger may seem an obvious step in an aggressive growth strategy. The catch is that the core passion surrounding the original business often does not translate into the new one. If the film manufacturer were inspired by a passion for photography, then it might do well in the camera world. If the airline were motivated by a desire to facilitate travel in any form, it might thrive as a full-service travel agency. If the fast food business were dedicated to bringing inexpensive food to the masses, then it might do just as well with pizza, tacos, or egg rolls as it did with burgers.

There are many instances, however, when there is no apparent relationship between merging businesses. An oil manufacturer may swallow up a producer of panty hose. A soft drink company may take over an entertainment business. A media conglomerate may engulf a toy company. In these instances I just shake my head and wonder what these companies are thinking. Organizations excel in those areas they are passionate about, not those that will simply add more revenue or diversify their activities. Alliances of this sort may in rare cases work; but just as a marriage based on convenience or appearance is apt to end in divorce, so is a merger of businesses that do not share an underlying love for what they do.

The final way that organizations lose sight of passion is that they never experience it to begin with. Some businesses are founded on pragmatics rather than emotion. Maybe Uncle Ray, who owns a meatpacking business, convinces you to rent a truck and start making deliveries for him. Perhaps you can't handle all the deliveries yourself, so you lease a few trucks and hire some college kids to drive at night. Before you know it, you may be the head of a small trucking firm, despite the fact that you don't care a bit about trucks or deliveries.

Many businesses start this way. Their purpose is to meet an immediate need. Perhaps the founders need quick income.

Maybe they want to appease insistent relatives. Or perhaps there is a glaring need in the community for a service they can easily provide. Whatever the case, the businesses they build will be lacking—in enthusiasm, in quality, in value. Some may grow; they may even be highly profitable. They might make the founders wealthy, put food on the tables of employees, and help customers get what they need, but will anyone really get what they want? The owners might be counting the days until they can retire or sell out. The employees may be cursing management under their breath and secretly searching for better jobs elsewhere. The customers might be willing to pay only as long as there is no competition or the price is low enough.

Building "Profit with a Capital P"

A case such as this does not highlight the benefits of passion I have already described—the ones that make businesses flow and enable them to succeed. Organizations can survive and even grow without it. Rather it demonstrates the most lasting and significant distinction that passion brings—what I call "Profit with a capital P." When organizations are built on passion, they don't just meet needs. They fulfill desires.

As I mentioned earlier, what qualifies as "success" in the business world is changing. The modern organization is focused on much more than the columns of its monthly profit and loss statements. Whatever is important to the organization, whatever result it hopes to achieve, that defines its Profit. This definition may include financial success but is likely to involve much more. A pharmaceutical company may define its Profit in terms of improving lives, both of the consumers who take its medications and the employees who manufacture them. An automobile manufacturer might qualify its Profit in terms of contributions made to the field of auto design, valuing recognition and awards over market share. One law firm may measure its success in terms of cases won and lost, while another might define Profit in terms of achieving social change.

Profit is not just an objective, though. Objectives can be temporary; they can be changed or discarded as time goes by. Profit is more significant and lasting than that. It is also not a stopping point or an all-or-nothing proposition. If the socially committed law firm were forced to close its doors today, having met only a few of its many objectives, it might still have realized its Profit. It might have increased public awareness, empowered some needy clients, and improved the abilities of its associates to seek change through other avenues. Just because it is no longer in operation does not mean it has not had an impact.

Ultimately Profit is the reason any organization exists. Whether it realizes its Profit—and achieves success on its own terms—will be determined largely by the role passion plays. This is true on the day-to-day level, as the organization derives fulfillment from where it is going, and also on the long-term level, as it finds meaning in its accomplishments.

Passion is the link between reality and Profit. An organization that aims to improve the lives of its employees is not going to achieve this goal if its leaders are not passionate about its programs and policies. A company that hopes to create world-class products will not be able to develop them if its associates are not excited about quality. A business that seeks to help customers will fall short if it is not eager to communicate with them. Even an organization that wants only to maximize its bottom line can do so only if everyone involved is emotionally committed to cost-cutting.

Passion Review

Profit with a Capital P is whatever is important to an organization, whatever results it hopes to achieve. It may imply financial success, but is likely to involve much more.

The Passion Scale™

Whether your organization is well on the road to Profit or has taken a detour along the way, it can use passion to fuel its progress, to achieve its most meaningful goals. It can join the ranks of the passioneers. For some this will require a radical change in outlook and operations, for others a simple refinement of existing focus or practices.

To help you assess your organization's current passion status, I want you to determine where it falls on the Passion Scale™. For each of the questions in Figure 1.1, rate the degree to which you agree with the statement on a scale from "10" (Always) to "0" (Never). Circle the appropriate answer. Use the key that follows to calculate a score.

	Always	Sometimes	Never
1. Positive emotion is present or felt throughout the organization.	10 9 8 7 6 5 4 3 2 1 0		
2. Leaders express or exude enthusiasm about the organization's work.	10 9 8 7 6 5 4 3 2 1 0		
3. The organization has identified the sources of its inspiration and/or the forces that drive its progress.	10 9 8 7 6 5 4 3 2 1 0		
4. These forces are articulated throughout the organization, from CEO to entry-level employee.	10 9 8 7 6 5 4 3 2 1 0		
5. The organization has a big purpose, vision, or mission that reflects these forces.	10 9 8 7 6 5 4 3 2 1 0		
6. Creativity and innovation are encouraged in the organization.	10 9 8 7 6 5 4 3 2 1 0		
7. Programs and policies are in place to educate associates about the organization and/or contribute to their personal growth.	10 9 8 7 6 5 4 3 2 1 0		
8. The organization is consistent in the direction and intent of its actions.	10 9 8 7 6 5 4 3 2 1 0		
9. Customers and partners are enthusiastic about their relationships with the organization.	10 9 8 7 6 5 4 3 2 1 0		
10. Employees, partners, and customers seek out the organization based on its reputation.	10 9 8 7 6 5 4 3 2 1 0		

Total Score _____

Figure 1.1. The Passion Scale.

Score	*Interpretation*
0–25	Passion-Devoid
26–50	Passion-Challenged
51–75	Passion-Building
76–100	Passion-Driven

If your organization scored between 0 and 25, it falls into the passion-devoid category. It is probably characterized by malaise, disgruntlement, unpredictability, high turnover, confusion, and poor performance. Very few organizations qualify as passion-devoid. Most exhibit some degree of passion, or they simply would not remain viable. The passion-devoid typically struggle to survive, go out of business, are shut down, or are radically restructured.

It is more likely that your organization scored somewhere between 26 and 75, and falls into either the passion-challenged or passion-building categories. A score of 26–50 indicates passion-challenged organizations. Such groups also suffer the negative effects of passion deficit but to a lesser degree. Chances are they preserve small pockets of passion that are sufficient to keep people involved and performance adequate. Though they survive, they benefit few in the organization. Passion-challenged organizations are characterized by ambivalence, frustration, inconsistency, moderate turnover, ambiguity, and mediocre performance.

Passion-building organizations score between 51 and 75 on the passion scale. They demonstrate a predisposition to passion that engages associates and empowers performance. They may or may not have programs in place to cultivate passion, but it flows nonetheless. The results are interest, encouragement, evenness, commitment, clarity, and productivity.

A score of 76–100 indicates a passion-driven organization. The passion-driven understand the power of passion, seek actively to build it, and reap the many rewards it offers. They are characterized by enthusiasm, excitement, constancy, loyalty, fulfillment, and prolificness. Figure 1.2 summarizes the effects of passion in the four types of organizations.

The Passion Scale can only be interpreted as a very rough indicator of your organization's need and readiness to create a "passion-driven" environment. The purpose of the scale is to

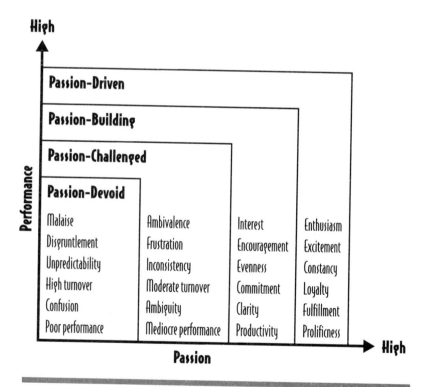

Figure 1.2. Effects of the Passion Scale.

help an organization begin the process of identifying leadership behaviors and organizational characteristics that may detract from becoming a "passion-driven" organization.

If you are part of an organization that seems hopeless, take heart. Even those that are uncertain of their Profit and devoid of passion can be transformed. If you are a CEO or founder, then the power for rapid and effective change truly resides in your hands. If you are a manager or front-line employee, the changes you can make will be less dramatic, but they will make a difference nonetheless. A single proponent of passion, a lone passioneer, can spark the changes that may eventually help turn around an entire organization.

If, on the other hand, you belong to an organization that is blazing a passion trail, consider yourself lucky and make it your business to understand the reasons for its success. The lessons you learn today will help you sustain the passion tomorrow and will enable you to make a difference in any organization you might join or create in the future.

If your organization falls somewhere in the middle, now might well be the perfect time for passion to come into play. So many businesses are poised on the verge of greatness but lack the edge they need to take them there. Let passion give your business that edge. Seek it out and cultivate it. Follow it to Profit.

The Passion Plan at Work

In the chapters that follow I will present a seven-step model for building a passion-driven organization. The plan will prove useful to any organization, regardless of where it falls on the

Passion Scale. In illustrating the concepts I present, I will high-light twelve organizations that have integrated passion into their day-to-day operations: Ben & Jerry's Homemade, Disney Institute, Gateway, GTE Directories, Brazosport Independent School District, Wainwright Industries, Clarke American, McLeodUSA, PSS/World Medical, EarthLink, MindSpring, and Southwest Airlines. Though none is perfect, each has recognized passion as a means of achieving Profit, of creating its own success.

As you read, remember this: in an increasingly competitive business environment, passion is a necessity. An organization that doesn't bring it to the table might as well walk away.

Passionism...

"To seize the benefits of passion, the organization must be engaged in activities that inspire it."

CHAPTER 2

Putting the Passion Plan to Work

A Model for Organizational Success

Give me where to stand and I will move the earth.
—Archimedes

Building a passion-driven organization is no simple challenge, but it can be both fun and rewarding. Fun? Yes, fun. Of the twelve organizations I studied for this book, more than half specify fun as an integral part of their business. This includes Southwest Airlines, a highly profitable organization that has gained a national reputation for its fun-loving spirit, and Ben & Jerry's, a widely respected organization committed to improving the world and having a good time while doing it. As company co-founder Jerry Greenfield says, "If it's not fun, why do it?" (Cohen and Greenfield, 1997, p. 20).

So as you prepare to bring passion into your organization, whether on an individual or organizational level, remember that above all you are committing yourself to a positive process:

you should be excited and prepared to have fun. Though the transformation may be involved, it should not be draining or depressing. If pursued carefully, it will be energizing and uplifting. It will invigorate the organization and its associates.

Why a Plan?

When I teach people about passion, some of the first questions they ask are "How can you plan the emotional?" "If passion is a natural, spontaneous force, how can you chart a course for experiencing it?" Passion is all of these things, but it can also be controlled, cultivated, and directed to achieve specific ends. This is especially important in the group setting, where passions must be shared to be effective.

Even in the organization where passion pervades, planning is critical to achieving productive ends. Consider the case of Apple Computer. In the early 1980s Apple seemed to exemplify passion. Led by the charismatic and passionate Steve Jobs, the company proclaimed a devotion to creating "insanely great" computers. For a few great years it pumped out technologically superior products that were innovative, stylish, and easy to use. Customers displayed an almost religious devotion to these products and were willing to pay a premium for them. Potential employees stormed the corporate offices in Cupertino, California, eager to be a part of the magic.

If you were to walk the halls of Apple back in those days, you would almost certainly have felt the passion. In fact it was the passion that began to undermine the organization and threaten its success. As documented in Jim Carlton's *Apple: The Inside Story of Intrigue, Egomania, and Business Blunders* (1997), the leaders of Apple were never able to control the passion that coursed through its corporate veins. While a love of technology was at the core of everything Apple did, the way that love was manifested took on different and opposing forms. Everyone was excited about the products: engineers were passionate about designing them, marketers were eager to package and promote them, and salespeople were excited about selling them. But somewhere in the mix, the entire group lost sight of why and how they were to accomplish these things.

Rather than articulating a clear and consistent strategy for channeling all this underlying passion, leadership allowed the various groups to develop their own interpretations, often at each other's expense. As a result employees became territorial and defensive. Viewing themselves as keepers of the flame, engineers felt it their right to demand excessive time and money in developing new products, apparently oblivious of the financial ramifications. Certain projects were given higher importance than others, and some even competed for resources and market position. By placing product groups at odds, leaders helped to create resentment and jealousies among fellow developers. Rather than sharing a passion for advancing the company's overall contribution to the world of computers, Apple's staff retreated into warring camps.

Sales and marketing employees resented the engineers' seeming control over the organization and often felt constrained in their roles. Fewer and fewer insanely great products rolled off the lines. In fact, many that emerged from the developers' dens were not even good. As the company began losing the technological edge it had claimed as its birthright, these employees lost their passion, as did many of the customers.

Apple's problems were complex. It is clear, however, that while passion gave the organization its edge in the early days, it later became its Achilles heel. From the beginning, the passion the organization possessed was bungled. Leaders used it to generate outstanding products, but then jealously guarded the company's accomplishments. They sought and encouraged it in employees, then left them to their own devices to clarify and manage it.

Ultimately, the organization had no long-term strategy for sustaining the passion that defined it. This lack of focus led to confusion in decision making, uncertainty in planning, and a series of costly tactical errors.

When Jobs, the original source of Apple's passion, was ousted in 1985, many thought things would calm down. People hoped that the more levelheaded approach of former Pepsi vice president John Sculley would put Apple on a steady course while retaining the intensity and enthusiasm Jobs had initiated. Ironically, Sculley and his series of successors were no more effective at channeling Apple's passion than Jobs had been.

As we enter the new millennium and what will certainly be a new era in personal computing, Steve Jobs has rejoined the Apple ranks as chief executive. With the hugely successful launch of its iMac series and a series of profitable improvements to its trademark operating system, Apple has experienced a rebirth. It looks like the company it once was, possessing a guiding passion for superior design and technology and a commitment to delivering it to customers.

If in the early days Jobs had foreseen the challenges that were to come, he most surely would have done things differently. He could have anticipated strengths and shortcomings of passion and defined a plan for developing and preserving it.

To help avoid such pitfalls, I urge organizations to invest significant time and energy in passion management. Whatever the scope of the changes required, they need to be taken on with care. An organization cannot simply hone in on a passion and run with it. It needs to consider where it wants that passion to lead it and how passion will take it there. It needs to remember that while passion has the power to distinguish, it also has the power to destroy. It is a force that merits respect and commands attention.

The Passion Plan at Work

The plan that follows provides a blueprint for approaching passion-based change in the organization. Each step is important, and none should be ignored. The steps are divided into three categories that reflect the sources from which they stem: feeling, thinking, and acting. I will briefly describe each category and step of the Passion Plan at Work here and then examine each in further detail in the chapters that follow.

A Note to Associates: Much of what you will read in this book is geared toward leaders. They are the ones who have the authority to implement change across the organization. By virtue of their position, they can make organization-wide changes more rapidly and effectively than can those who report to them. If you are not a "formal" leader in your organization or in a position to make changes that extend beyond your own performance, do not be disheartened. These steps are still critical to your personal path within your organization. Once you understand the fundamentals of passion-based change, you will be better prepared to manage your personal

Figure 2.1. The Passion Plan at Work Model™.

passion and make contributions that will help set a passion-driven tone in your organization. For detailed guidance on dealing with passion on an individual level, you can consult the first book in this series, *The Passion Plan: A Step-by-Step Guide to Discovering, Developing, and Living Your Passion.*

feeling

The first two steps in the plan—start from the heart and discover core passions—require leaders and associates to get in touch with the heart of the organization. To seize the benefits of passion, the organization must be engaged in activities that inspire it. It cannot simply accept its current direction and expect to graft passion on; it must feel first, and then determine where those feelings will lead.

Step One: Start From The Heart

Making the leap from being a reason-based organization to a passion-driven one can seem daunting. Leaders and associates must overcome the traditional biases against emotion in business (other than fierce competitiveness) and embrace passion as a source of success. They must begin to view the heart not as a source of weakness but as a reserve of hidden strength.

Those reluctant to enter uncharted emotional waters will be encouraged by the examples of the organizations highlighted in this book. All have distinguished themselves in their respective fields by proudly wearing their hearts on their sleeves. Rather than concealing their excitement, they have openly expressed it and found ways to capitalize on it. Unabashedly emotional in its operations and appeal, Southwest Airlines even listed itself on the New York Stock Exchange using the symbol LUV!

Step Two: Discover Core Passions

Many organizations have grown out of touch with the passions on which they were founded. Some have experienced changes of heart and focus in intervening years. Some have never given a thought to passion. To benefit from passion's power, the organization must first identify where its passions lie.

This challenge should fall to the leaders of the organization. It may involve identifying passions that already exist but have not been articulated, or defining new passions to be developed. As part of the discovery process, they must examine the forces that motivate them, both individually and collectively. They must evaluate the organization's current competencies and strengths as well as its potential for future growth. They then need to consider the feelings of employees and customers surrounding the business and look for connections between those emotions and company performance.

Using all this information, leaders can work together to create a Passion Profile™ of the organization. This profile will highlight potential core passions, or the ideas and activities that could be the focus of the organization's efforts. Again, these possible passions are not picked randomly out of a hat; they are a reflection of the current strengths and emotions of the organization and its associates. They emanate from the gut, not the head. They are instinctual, not contrived.

Sometimes leaders can be daunted by this task; they should not be. The profile is not an exercise in certainty, but rather a starting point for further inquiry. Once potential passions have been identified, the organization can find ways to explore them further and investigate the possibilities they offer.

For associates in organizations whose leaders have not identified core passions, discovering personal passions and identifying what excites them about their organization becomes particularly important. Even though they cannot unilaterally change the direction of the entire group, they can help to bring about change from the bottom up through their example and enthusiasm.

Thinking

Once leaders and associates have uncovered the heart of the organization and identified its core passions, they must begin to think as well as feel. They need to use reason to determine how these passions can best serve the organization. The next two steps—clarify purpose and define actions—ensure that as the organization begins to focus on passion, it will do so in ways that are both effective and meaningful.

Step Three: Clarify Purpose

If I were to start a business today based on my passion for golf, I would face many choices as to what direction that business would take. No matter how strong my passion, I would have to decide my purpose in pursuing it. What would be the reason for the new organization's existence? It might be to increase public awareness of the sport, to provide equipment to participants, or to design world-class courses. In making my decision, I would have to consider many factors and use my judgment to determine the best alternative. I would employ reason to give shape to my passion, not to undermine it.

Most organizations have a purpose by default. Something has defined their current activities—market needs, leadership desires, or consultants' advice. Often, however, their purpose does not reflect any underlying passion, which leads to lack of focus and poor performance. A chocolate company started a century ago originally devoted itself to creating high-quality, elegant confections based on traditional European recipes and techniques. Under pressure to produce higher profit margins, the company has gradually changed its focus from producing quality to pumping out quantity. While the passion for chocolate that inspired the business can still be found in pockets of the organization, it has been largely undermined, as employees and customers alike have lost pride in the product. Profits have resulted, but so have dissatisfaction and instability.

Consider also the reverse of this example. A few college kids motivated by a passion for junk food start a chocolate company. Their self-proclaimed mission is to line the shelves of every university snack shop with cheap and tasty treats. They are wildly successful. High-priced advisers recommend they move into gourmet confections to be marketed at coffeehouses and upscale supermarkets. They make the change but both the products and the company lose their luster. The excitement and fun generated by creating inexpensive "brain food" for young adults have fallen victim to more sedate and arguably boring pursuits.

Each of these cases demonstrates why clarifying purpose is such an important step. Whether the business is in its infancy or an aging relic in need of revitalization, it must define its reasons for existing—the direction it will take and the ends it will serve. If purpose is in alignment with the core passions of the organization, it will provide a viable means of pursuing and sustaining them.

Associates must likewise determine the purpose they find in performing their jobs. While individual employees cannot simply decide the purpose of the organization, they can identify the rationale for their own work. A single associate dedicated to pleasing customers can start a customer service movement from within based on personal accomplishment and resulting influence.

Step Four: Define Actions

After leaders have clearly defined what fuels the organization (its passions) and where it will go using that fuel (its purpose), they need to create a plan for getting there. They cannot hope that passion, once unleashed, will catapult the organization to greatness. It certainly can, but it probably won't without careful attention to the ways and times it will be used.

An action plan has three basic elements: the long-term plan, the short-term plan, and the contingency plan. Collectively these elements plot potential courses for passion-based change. They target specific actions for introducing, developing, and strengthening passion in the organization, and prescribe the scope, intensity, and pace of change to be pursued.

While it nails down distinct courses of action, the plan is not written in stone. It is a dynamic, living document subject to adaptation as the organization progresses. This flexibility is critical as passion grows in the organization. Often the increased motivation and ability passion provides create unforeseen opportunities, which should not be ruled out simply because they were not anticipated in the planning stage.

Associates can create their own action plans for change within their individual positions or departments. Often plans that work for one person or one group become the model for the entire organization.

Acting

Once the organization is confident in both its passion and its purpose and is equipped with a plan, it is prepared to act. Planning for change and actually bringing it about are of course two different things. Whereas the previous stages— feeling and thinking—required hypothetical courage, acting requires the organization to actually put its money where its mouth is. Leaders and associates must be prepared to move forward with conviction and without regret. This requires commitment, enthusiasm, and persistence, all of which will further the organization on its road to Profit.

Step Five: Perform With Passion

If leaders have undertaken the discovery and planning processes privately, the changes they introduce may come as a shock to those both inside and outside the organization. Even if employees are aware of changes in advance, they might not be prepared to accept or benefit from them. To ensure that the transition will work, it is critical that as plans are deployed the organization be truly aligned in its efforts. The leaders must not only introduce change, they must also exemplify it. They must work to create an environment in which the core passions will thrive and in which associates of the organization can perform passionately.

Leaders can do many things to facilitate smooth and effective change. The first and most important is to clearly and constantly communicate the organization's core passions and their plans for integrating them into the business. They can make improvements to the physical surroundings to allow associates to express their passion and maximize their performance. They can also refine policies and practices to promote passion-based productivity rather than hinder it.

Associates seeking to make changes at the individual level can also take steps to create a passion-inspiring environment for themselves. Within the bounds of their authority, they can adapt their workspaces, habits, and activities to elicit personal passion and build it in those around them.

As the organization begins to change and improve, it will truly begin to perform with passion. Leaders will learn to make passion-informed decisions and to "let go" while employees use their freedom to build on core passions and make further improvements. The organization will become self-motivated and increasingly capable. The engines of success will begin to work from within, with little need for outside guidance or inspiration.

Step Six: Spread Excitement

As the organization begins to act with passion, it will gain notice. The passionate shine like beacons in a world where most face frustration and dissatisfaction. Many organizations and individuals that consider themselves successful realize there is something more they are lacking. They are secretly aware they are failing to reach their potential. By actively spreading its passion, the passion-driven organization can help these groups and fuel its own progress in the process.

This may sound far-fetched, but think of it in these terms. If a software training company is driven by a passion to empower people through computer skills, is it better served by sharing its enthusiasm or concealing it? The answer is obvious. If employees "catch the fever" and are inspired by their work, they will be more effective in teaching their clients. If clients witness this excitement firsthand, they will be more likely to learn and to request future help from the company. Energetic employees may attract other qualified, enthusiastic trainers who can contribute their passion to the organization. Trainees might spread the word about the company to other potential clients. Through the added attention and excitement, the organization might gain media coverage or industry recognition.

This is the snowball effect of passion. Once it begins to roll, it picks up speed and takes others along for the ride. But they are not taken unwillingly. They are eager to join and partake of the energy passion creates. Ultimately they might be inspired to discover their own passions, but the immediate effect is that they strengthen the organization by sharing and upholding its passion.

Organizations that are sensitive to this effect can seek to capitalize on it. They can implement programs internally to help employees use and develop their personal passions. They can reach out to customers and educate them in the passions of the organization. They can find ways to increase awareness of their practices among their colleagues and even their competitors. This is true because the passion-driven company does not fear its competition; it is always one step ahead. By raising the level of performance across its field, the passion-driven organization perpetuates its own commitment to sustaining its passion and its edge.

Associates in non-passion-driven organizations will find that expressing their passion and sharing it with others in the group can have a similar effect. They can influence leaders, customers, and coworkers in ways that contribute to the growth of passion across the organization. After all, a single spark can ignite a firestorm.

Step Seven: Stay The Course

Usually organizations that begin to make passion-based change are uplifted. Much to their surprise, they often find the changes easier than they anticipated and are energized by their efforts. Even so they must be certain not to be carried away by their successes. They must remain close to the passion that inspired them and seek diligently to preserve it.

The same holds true for those that find change difficult. Sometimes it seems easier to abandon a new course of action than to sustain the energy necessary to follow it. If employees or customers resist, then leaders might be tempted to return to their old ways. Though they should reevaluate their plan based on these reactions, they should not turn away from their passion. Perhaps they have not communicated effectively or provided sufficient opportunities for associates to grow. Whatever the case, a change in tactics does not necessitate a change of heart. Passion must predominate! This is true for associates seeking to make changes at the individual level as well. Both the organization and the individual must remain committed; they must stay the course in order to reach their Profit.

Passion Review

Phases of the Passion Plan:

Feel	*Think*	*Act*
• Start From The Heart	• Clarify Purpose	• Perform With Passion
• Discover Core Passions	• Define Actions	• Spread Excitement
		• Stay The Course

A Return to Profit

If the organization remains true to its passion and follows these seven steps, it will find the results it seeks, whether the results are measured in dollars, awards, or accomplishments. As it does, it will also discover some unexpected benefits, because passion can take organizations to another level. It can open worlds and expand horizons. It can bring new awareness and heightened perceptions. It can empower and improve.

In the chapters that follow I will show you how to take the steps necessary to transform any organization from passionless to passionate. While leaders have the greatest potential for introducing sweeping change, associates at all levels can make a difference. Regardless of your position, you will learn ways to bring passion into your organization, to build it, and to benefit from it. So read on and begin your quest to build a passion-driven organization!

Passionism...

"When the heart is ignored or suppressed, the result is the same for the organization as it is for the individual: unrealized potential."

CHAPTER 3

Step One: Start from the Heart

Passion as the Foundation of the Organization's Success

One sees clearly only with the heart. Anything essential is invisible to the eyes.
—ANTOINE DE SAINT-EXUPERY, *THE LITTLE PRINCE*

For passion to be effective, it must be the foundation of the organization. It cannot be an accessory or a technique that is called upon in times of trouble or remembered periodically at anniversaries and corporate milestones. It has to be the starting point from which all else—purpose, vision, culture, strategy, policies, and practices—emanates. This requires organizations and the individuals who lead them to possess a unique attitude toward business and life. They must be intensely aware of their motivations and committed not only to pursuing them but also to excelling in their pursuit. They must start from the heart.

This attitude does not come naturally to many organizations or their associates. To begin operating with passion, they must confront obstacles and defy limitations they themselves have imposed. Only when they have broken down such barriers can they begin to view the world through the lens of passion and claim the advantages it provides.

The Heart-First Organization

In my work with organizations I have witnessed a growing trend. Although many successful businesses are grounded in expertise, just as many are founded upon a strong desire to achieve a specific social end. These organizations truly operate from the heart. Technical considerations, manufacturing and equipment issues, and administrative concerns are all important, but they are secondary to the core passions that drive the business.

Consider the case of McLeodUSA. In the late 1970s founder Clark McLeod was a middle school teacher in his hometown of Cedar Rapids, Iowa. He felt the itch of the entrepreneurial bug and around 1980 decided he would start of all things a long distance company. This had only recently become a possibility with the breakup of Ma Bell, and to McLeod it seemed an area ripe with opportunity. McLeod built his company, eventually called Telecom*USA, from scratch. Not many would have wagered that a teacher from a small town in the Midwest could create a billion-dollar enterprise. But those who joined McLeod in his efforts were richly rewarded in 1990, when he sold Telecom*USA to MCI for $1.25 billion.

Millions in pocket, McLeod could have retired to a beach in the Caribbean, but he was not content to sit idly and watch his fortune grow. He was passionate about putting his wealth to work for others. With his wife, Mary, he created a family foundation that made sizable and frequent contributions to various charitable and cultural organizations. The McLeods were frustrated by how little their money accomplished in the hands of these groups and decided to do something different.

Clark wanted to create something that would endure, an organization that would not just drop money into the community, but would actually fuel economic progress. He decided he would start another business. He didn't know what type of business it would be, but that didn't really matter. What did matter was that the company be devoted to "creating spectacular opportunities" for individuals. By providing employees with such chances, he could create an organization that would really make a difference. The company would be an economic engine in the community, creating salaries that would feed back into other businesses. It would prioritize community involvement and provide opportunities for employees to contribute on both a personal and group level.

McLeod was just as prepared to accept opportunity as he was to offer it. When he learned that the state of Iowa was going to build an extensive fiber optic network, he contacted some of his old colleagues and proposed that they throw their hats in the ring. The two-year non-compete agreement he had signed with MCI had expired and he was ready to build on his previous success. McLeod won the contract and was hired to construct and maintain the new network.

Today McLeodUSA employs over nine thousand people and provides selected integrated telecommunications services to customers nationwide. The organization is committed to being the number one and the most admired company in the communities it serves, but is driven by its passion for creating something truly great—a lasting, successful organization that allows individuals and communities to thrive and grow.

Heart-first organizations like McLeodUSA exist and succeed because of passion. If they were reluctant to acknowledge the importance of the forces that motivate them, they would become just another company. What makes them different is that they give precedence to their passion. They make it a priority. They are willing to take risks to follow it. Clark McLeod recently wrote, "Risk is inherent in life . . . standing still is the riskiest life of all. . . . The risk associated with the climb allows us to experience the thrill of living that those left behind may never feel" (McLeod, 2000, p. 180).

McLeod is so impressed by the power of passion that he and the leaders of the company have made it one of the organization's core values—along with growth, relationships, and integrity. Employees are encouraged to express their passion on the job and evaluated on their ability to do so. A Passion Team exists that plans activities and events to spread the company's passion to the community.

The Risks of Passion

McLeodUSA is a pioneer in passion management. From its inception, its leaders have recognized the advantages passion offers and have strived to build a business based on those strengths. The organization abounds with passion while so many others have none. But why is this? Why are so many organizations reluctant or unwilling to start from the heart? Why do so many suffer from what I call passion deficit?

As Clark McLeod highlighted, *passion is risky*. On an individual level, many are frightened to put themselves out on a limb to pursue the things that really matter to them. They feel vulnerable and exposed in doing so. By pursuing their dreams, they open themselves up to criticism, misunderstanding, and in the worst case, failure. The same holds true at the organizational level. Passion has not been established in textbooks as a fail-safe business practice. Starting a business based on personal passions, infusing it with one's ideals and dreams, is scary stuff. Even the toughest entrepreneur can crumble under the scrutiny of outside critics when the heart is on the line. It is easier to weather the scrutiny and if necessary abandon ship if the heart is not invested. Walking away, though difficult, is not tantamount to personal defeat.

For established businesses, the challenge of emotional involvement can seem equally daunting. Maintaining the status quo, which may be less than ideal, often seems less threatening than making a change. To many, aligning a business around passion seems like entering the great unknown. The prospect of appearing weak or foolish scares leaders into sticking with their safer head-based strategies. Ironically, it also prevents them from experiencing the strength and success passion can bring.

The benefits of passion are available only to those willing to actively seek them. Organizations must be prepared to take a chance if they want to raise their performance to a higher level, if they want to become truly great businesses. Contrary to what some might believe, passion does not necessarily create capricious or irresponsible organizations; when used wisely it builds smart, gutsy businesses that bring about success on their own terms.

Symptoms of Passion Deficit

You probably have a pretty good idea of where your organization stands with regard to passion. If it is like most, it could stand to improve its passion practices. If you are uncertain, take a moment to consider the symptoms of passion deficit. They are easy to recognize and all too common in today's organizations. At their most extreme, they characterize what I defined in Chapter One as the passion-devoid, the cold fish of the business world. On a lower level, they signify a loss of intensity and potential. Most stem from leadership but spread quickly to all levels of the organization. If exhibited consistently, they define the outlook and actions of the business. These are the most notable:

Apathy. An absence of passion often results in an absence of emotion. Associates of the organization seem not to care whether it fails or succeeds. They do their work, collect a paycheck, and hope for little more. Leaders may be "retired on the job," waiting around only long enough for their options to vest or their retirement plans to kick in. While apathy does not necessarily result in a negative environment, it prevents the organization from growing or improving.

Frustration. If associates retain an emotional connection to their work, a lack of passion at the organizational level can prove highly frustrating. They find the individual passion they bring to the job stifled and their efforts underappreciated. Leaders and employees alike find themselves bucking a system that does not recognize or sustain their intensity. This atmosphere of frustration is reinforced when the organization's collective efforts consistently fall short or are ineffective.

Contention. With emotion still in play on the individual level and no core passion defined at the group level, passion deficit can create an atmosphere of contention in the organization. Associates develop their own interpretations of where the organization is going and fight vehemently over how to get there. Lacking a commitment to a common passion, their efforts are counterproductive and produce feelings of hostility and resentment. Subsequently the organization is crippled by infighting.

Confusion. When passion is not communicated or promoted in the organization, associates get confused. There might be a professed mission or vision, but with no emotion or conviction to back it up, what should be done remains unclear. Employees do not know what to expect, and leaders do not know what to reward. Progress is difficult, if not impossible, because there is no galvanizing force or direction to the organization.

Low Morale. These symptoms, working separately or in combination, drain morale from the organization. After enduring any one for too long, associates become defeated. Some resign themselves to their lot, while others (usually the most motivated and valuable) move on. Those who stay have little faith in the organization and lose incentive to perform.

Ineffectiveness. When passion is missing, people find it difficult to focus and even harder to perform. Goals are set but rarely met. Guidelines are established but rarely followed. The implications for the organization are significant. It becomes ineffective—unable to meet its commitments or uphold its standards. Leaders and employees feel inadequate and the business is not respected.

Inconsistency. An organization that is out of touch with its heart often gets lost on the road to success. Without an underlying passion to fuel its progress or define its efforts, it does not produce consistent results. Associates find energy in fits and spurts, and leadership vacillates in its initiatives. The atmosphere in the organization changes from week to week, as does the quality of work the organization produces.

Poor Performance. An inability to succeed on any terms is a sure sign that passion is missing or working ineffectively in an organization. If associates are enthusiastic and motivated, performance will, at a minimum, be good. When passion is completely absent, organizations can be plagued by consistent problems with productivity, quality, and commitment. Once these problems take root, they are difficult to erase.

A Return to the Heart

To overcome these obstacles to success, the organization must change its perspective. It does not need to be grounded in lofty social goals or inspired to change the world, but *it must start from the heart.* This entails a new awareness and also a commitment to breaking down the barriers that are keeping passion out of the organization.

A New Awareness

We are creatures of emotion. No matter what we may do to deny our feelings or fight them off, they remain. More important, they inspire us to act the way we do and cause us to experience life in our own unique way. Symbolically we say our emotions stem from the heart. We claim it to be the source of all feeling and the possessor of our true identity. If we are not true to what is in our hearts, then we betray ourselves and deny our potential.

Organizations are human in nature. Like the people who build them, they possess emotion and have a spirit that defines them. Simply stated, they have a heart. When that heart is ignored or suppressed, the result is the same for the organization as it is for the individual: unrealized potential.

Passion Review

Symptoms of Passion Deficit

Apathy	Low Morale
Frustration	Ineffectiveness
Contention	Inconsistency
Confusion	Poor Performance

Only when we experience emotion do we experience life in its fullness. We could go through our days oblivious to ups and downs, warding off both pain and pleasure, but what would we have to show for it? Would we know excitement? Would we accomplish anything spectacular?

Just as we should not fear our hearts and the emotions they unleash, nor should the organization. The people who set its tone and determine its direction should not strive to make it dispassionate or sober. Those who do its work should not be afraid to bring their energy and enthusiasm to the table. Nothing and no one is served by denying the forces that breathe life, creativity, and energy into a group.

Luckily the mistaken notion that efficiency is a byproduct of dullness is rapidly disappearing from today's marketplace. Slowly but surely business is coming to the realization that there is strength rather than weakness in emotion. Employees thrive on it; customers yearn for it. But just because the obvious is finally becoming obvious does not mean leaders know what to make of it.

To help people understand how emotion can be a vital force in the business world, and how an awareness of its power can build a great organization, I need mention only one word: Disney. From the time he founded the company that bears his name, Walt Disney sought to create magic through entertainment. First it was through animation, later through theme parks. He dreamed of bringing happiness to children and adults alike and knew that to realize this dream, his employees must share his passion and pour their hearts into their work.

More than seventy-five years later, the Walt Disney Company has become one of the world's most beloved and successful businesses. The sight of the Disney logo or the spires of the Magic Kingdom kindles fond feelings within all its visitors. We have a deep emotional response to the company because it has worked for so long to win our trust and to consistently provide us with enjoyable experiences.

Walt Disney achieved this success because he focused on the heart. At the personal level he heeded his dream of providing high-quality family entertainment at a time when others thought him foolish. On the organizational level, he built a business that not only required passion in its employees but also nurtured it in them. Associates of the organization had a keen awareness of what was expected of them. They knew their focus was creating a meaningful and memorable experience for their "guests," whether theater patrons or vacationers.

Disney has expanded far beyond its origins, moving in recent decades into publishing, television, and the Internet, but its core passions have remained the same: it is still driven by a desire to create magical and meaningful experiences. It recognizes the importance of emotion in life and seeks to inspire it in its customers and employees.

One of Disney's more recent enterprises is the Disney Institute, a 117-acre campus and spa located in the Walt Disney World Resort in Orlando, Florida. This organization is dedicated explicitly to helping individuals explore their passions and to spreading the Disney organization's passion for creating a "guest experience" to other companies.

The Institute was the brainchild of Disney CEO Michael Eisner. After visiting Chatauqua, a summer educational community located in upstate New York, Eisner realized that Disney needed an educational community of its own, a place that would provide substantive learning experiences for its guests. While the institute he envisioned would focus on education and the arts, it would be different than other similar organizations. It would deliver these experiences to its guests in a uniquely Disney way.

Today the Disney Institute offers myriad programs designed to provide opportunities for personal growth and enrichment. Promotional literature claims that by taking a break from their routines, visitors can ignite "their passion for learning." The Institute suggests a variety of approaches for achieving this, including "immersing yourself in the field you love" while surrounded by "people who share your passions." Another is "trying things that are new and totally different," an experience that might help visitors discover hidden passions.

Like McLeodUSA, the Disney Institute exemplifies a heart-first organization. Its origins stem from passion, as do its objectives. Its motto is "You won't believe what you can do." This is the same message I deliver to individuals and organizations alike. With passion behind you, you are capable of more than you ever imagined.

Training sessions for corporate clients held at the Institute focus on themes such as "winning the hearts of employees," leaders "inspiring" their followers and "creating the magic" for customers. The last seminar highlights the "crucial point at which customers develop an emotional attachment to the organization," the hallmark of Disney's achievement.

Passion pervades the Institute. Employees are selected and trained based on their commitment and enthusiasm for its core passions. They are encouraged to develop their own passions in ways that will benefit guests and contribute to their personal growth. Guests are given opportunities to discover and explore their passions while also indulging in the comfort that such a guest-centered environment provides.

What the Disney Institute illustrates vividly and in so many ways is the critical awareness that organizations and the individuals that make them must have: the power to realize Profit stems from the heart. In the words of the Institute, organizations won't believe what they can achieve if only they let passion in. With this awareness, they are able to welcome passion, to embrace it, and to use it!

Breaking Down the Deterrents to Passion

Of course awareness alone is not enough to bring about change. Before they begin to bring passion in, leaders must work to break down the deterrents that are keeping it out. Such barriers include, but are not limited to, the following:

Fear. Associates cannot be afraid to make changes or to take risks in order to move the organization to a higher level. Leaders must drive fear out of the workplace by creating a safe environment in which passion is supported and encouraged. If they feel strengthened on an individual level, associates can stand together to endure any criticism that might come from outsiders.

Doubt. Associates might be equally daunted if they doubt the organization's ability to improve or change. If leaders have conveyed a mood of skepticism or a lack of confidence in the organization's potential, they must work diligently to reverse it. Leaders must exude a firm belief in and excitement about its present abilities and future possibilities.

Numbness. If an organization has been headed in a given direction for a long time without progressing or changing, its associates might be deadened emotionally. They might have lost their sense of what matters and be "going through the motions" in their work. To combat this, leaders must revitalize the organization by building emotion back into it. They can do this by bringing emotion into their jobs and creating events and opportunities that elicit it in others.

Self-limiting behavior. Organizations that are not confident in their abilities often find excuses to prevent testing them. The prevailing mood becomes, "We can't, because . . . ." When associates are accustomed to seeing the organization by way of its limitations and not its capabilities, it is hard for them to feel passionate about its potential. In this case, leaders must communicate a positive vision of new possibilities. They must encourage employees to challenge their perceptions and look for opportunities rather than excuses.

Caution. Sometimes organizations want to rest on their laurels. They don't want to jeopardize what they have already gained, and as a result are overly cautious in their actions. Associates learn to view opportunities as threats to the status quo and so are not eager to pursue them. More important, in this guarded environment, they are unlikely to be excited about their work or the organization. Leaders must promote a spirit of boldness and encourage associates to push the boundaries of what has been considered "safe."

Procrastination. Some organizations know change is necessary, but find ways to continually postpone it. This may result from laziness or uncertainty, but whatever its source, it impedes progress and stifles passion. If a "we'll-do-it-tomorrow" attitude pervades the organization, leaders must immediately inform associates that tomorrow has finally come. Though the specifics may be undetermined, the change in attitude is enough to empower the organization to begin moving forward and letting passion in.

Any and all of these things can be done even before the organization has defined its core passions. In fact, the more steps the organization takes toward creating a passion-friendly environment, the smoother the transition will be when an action plan is implemented. Regardless of the direction the organization decides to take, it can begin building excitement and energy around the concepts of potential and opportunity. If associates form an emotional connection to the organization, if they sense it has a heart, they will be eager and prepared to take part in building its future.

If you are an associate who wants to instigate passion-based change in your organization, the same barriers exist. But you must fight them on a personal level. Though you might not have the support of your leaders, you can begin to make a difference by overcoming your own fears and limitations. By waking up to your potential, approaching your work with renewed confidence and enthusiasm, testing your limits, and taking risks, you can open the door for passion in your work and show others how to do the same.

Passion Review

Deterrents to Passion
- Fear
- Doubt
- Numbness
- Self-limiting behavior
- Caution
- Procrastination

Start Today

The most important aspect of Step One is immediacy. No matter how broad the scope, how strong the intensity, or how rapid the pace of the changes required to transform the organization, it can commit to starting from the heart *today*. It may be the easiest or most difficult step to take depending on the history of the organization and the mind-set of its associates.

Whether you are an owner, a leader, or an associate, you can begin the change now. Rather than erecting all the traditional barriers by asking why—why take a risk, why push the limits, why enter the unknown—ask why not. Why not make the changes that will empower and uplift the organization? Why not capitalize on the most valuable and readily available source of success? Why not begin building tomorrow's Profit today? Start from the heart, and prepare to let the passion in!

PASSION PLAN WORKSHEET #1

Step One: Start from the Heart	How
A. "High Priority" Passion Sources:	List examples that accurately and clearly describe specific situations or times when the organization's CEO or top executives were • Thrilled to be leading the organization • Exuberant • Enthralled • Exhilarated • Experiencing rushes of enthusiasm Note: Situations and experiences that repeatedly elicit feelings like those listed above are typically "higher priority" sources of passion for the organization.

Passion Plan Worksheet #1 (cont.)

B. Primary Passion-Deficit Symptoms:

Symptom   *Why Exist?*

What symptoms of passion-deficit, if any, are present in the organization's culture? Why do the symptoms exist? Symptoms may include (but are not limited to) the following:

- Apathy
- Frustration
- Contention
- Confusion
- Low morale
- Ineffectiveness
- Inconsistency
- Poor performance

Passionism...

"Core passions define the heart of the organization. They are nonnegotiable."

CHAPTER 4

Step Two: Discover Core Passions

Uncovering the Forces That Will Drive the Organization's Success

You can't wait for inspiration. You have to go after it with a club.
—JACK LONDON

Is your business driven by passion? Is there an inherent excitement in the organization about its activities and direction? Do associates possess a clear vision of what the group is trying to achieve and why? If the answers to these questions are anything less than an emphatic yes, then the organization is probably out of touch with passion on some level. Whether there are hints of passion here and there or it is completely lacking, the next step in creating a passion-driven organization is uncovering the forces that have the potential to inspire the organization's associates and guide its progress.

I call these forces *core passions*. They are the ideas and activities that define the heart of the organization, whether they are acted upon or not. When the distractions imposed by outsiders and the obstacles created by insiders are stripped away, they are the things that truly matter. They breathe life and excitement into the organization and, if utilized, can fuel its success.

The heart-first organization is acutely aware of its core passions and is actively engaged in pursuing them. On the contrary, those that are head-first in their approach usually have lost sight of their passions or have become unclear as to where they really lie. These organizations must take the step of discovering (or possibly rediscovering) their core passions. This is crucial: even if leaders have committed to start from the heart, their passion for change is not enough. There must be more. There must be substance to the change. Only when they have identified the passions that are unique to their organization—the ones that truly define it—can they begin to build on them and bring about effective and lasting change.

Passion Review

Core passions are the ideas and activities that define the heart of the organization. They are nonnegotiable.

Ways to Discover Passion

The process of discovery is an exciting and often unpredictable one. It can occur in many ways and at many times during the life of an organization. Though later in the chapter

I will present some specific steps leaders can take to facilitate the process, I want to first describe some of the ways it can occur spontaneously.

Discovery by Epiphany

In 1991 Wainwright Industries was an award-winning organization. Dedicated to engineering, stamping, machining, and assembling metal products, the small family-owned operation in St. Peters, Missouri, consistently delivered high-quality goods to the automotive and aerospace industries. Despite the apparent success, all was not perfect at Wainwright. It had embarked on a quality-improvement initiative ten years earlier, and though the quality of the products had improved, the processes and environment that generated those products had not.

Mike Simms, plant manager, was on the verge of quitting. He was frustrated by the Wainwright management's attitude toward its employees. Decisions came from the top: rank and file team associates were not trusted to be part of the process. Though the owners had been investigating methods for improving their leadership practices, they had not incorporated any substantive changes into their management style.

This was the situation when in January 1991, Simms and other members of the management team attended a presentation by a vice president of IBM Rochester, which had just won the Malcolm Baldrige National Quality Award. As the speaker outlined the sources of IBM's accomplishments, six words stuck in Mike Simms's mind: "sincere trust and belief in people." He jotted the words down on a napkin and began asking the other leaders whether it existed at Wainwright. They all realized immediately it did not.

This was a moment of awakening for Wainwright Industries. Though highly skilled at what it did, there was something missing from its operations. There was no passion behind its professed commitment to quality, and this lack of passion was reflected in management's mood and strategy. As Chairman and CEO Don Wainwright told me, "Talk about dumb management. We were really stupid. We were a bunch of idiot managers who didn't understand that trust and belief comes not from the people to us, but from us to the people. We were saying one thing and our systems were saying just the opposite." In other words, the commitment to improvement had taken place on a technical level but not on an emotional one. The hearts of the Wainwright associates were not engaged in their quest.

On that day the Wainwright management team discovered a core passion that would transform its culture and lead it to win the Baldrige award only three years later. Don Wainwright was so moved by his new awareness that he stood before his employees and apologized for failing them. He vowed to trust and believe in them and by so doing make them an integral part of the company's progress. He backed up his claim by investing millions of dollars in employee training programs and rewarding individuals for making improvements on their own initiative.

This change has empowered the organization to pursue its commitment to excellence and total customer satisfaction; in fact it has transformed what before were mathematical objectives into passions that are carried out on a daily basis by each and every employee. Team Wainwright associates make thousands of improvements to the organization's operations every year. These improvements are closely monitored and measured—but they are not about numbers, they are about feelings. They reflect the pride, empowerment, and inspiration that now underlie the organization.

Today Wainwright Industries is recognized worldwide for superior products, an unparalleled safety record, and stellar customer satisfaction ratings. It is also recognized as a leader in employee performance and teamwork initiatives. None of these accomplishments would have been possible had it not been for that fateful day when Mike Simms, Don Wainwright, and the other Wainwright leaders were jolted into an awareness of what then was a weakness, but immediately became a passion. Sincere trust and belief in people is the foundation of the company and truly fuels its success.

Wainwright's was a discovery of passion by epiphany: a single pivotal experience made the leaders suddenly and intensely aware of it. The experience was unexpected and powerful.

Most organizations do not encounter such "aha" moments, but they can happen almost anytime and anywhere. As part of their commitment to start from the heart, leaders must be in tune with their emotions and the underlying emotions of the organization. Though they cannot anticipate an epiphany, they can be open to the possibility and sensitive to the feelings that will define it. This will prepare them not only to recognize an undiscovered passion but also to embrace it and act upon it.

Discovery Through Change

Epiphany reveals truth instantaneously. It is an eye-opening and heart-moving experience, and its implications are clear. Discovery through change occurs not as a major event itself but as a response to one. Events such as the loss of a critical contract, the death of a leader, and the emergence of a new competitor can rock the foundations of a business and force it to examine its direction. As leaders evaluate the impact of such changes and look for ways to respond, they might uncover existing passions or discover new ones.

This was the case with GTE Directories Corporation. A leading Yellow Pages publisher for over fifty years, the company nestled comfortably in its niche market with little competition to threaten its prominence. That changed in the 1980s, however, as new forms of media and a new group of publishers began taking over much of its business. Advertisers had new alternatives and began to question the effectiveness of their relationship with GTE Directories.

Realizing that it had to respond to the significant change that was occurring in the marketplace, the organization began interviewing customers. Leaders hoped to learn what it was they could and should be doing to keep their business alive. What they learned shocked them. As one employee relates, "[Prior to that time] we were an arrogant company. We knew what the customer wanted and we told them what they needed. But when we conducted focus groups in the late 1980s and early 1990s we were dismayed to hear how our customers perceived our attitude. Instead of being impressed by our knowledge, products, and service, they were intimidated. We had forgotten to listen to them, recognize their business needs, and develop a business relationship with them."

In the wake of such feedback, executives realized that sweeping change was necessary. They carefully investigated their options and, like Wainwright, began to feel as well as think. They understood that if they wanted to keep customers, they had to be passionate about meeting their needs. They vowed to go beyond just meeting needs and committed to "delighting" those they serve—an odd choice of words for a publishing company, but one that reflects the inherently emotional nature of the supplier-customer relationship.

The vision GTE Directories articulated to its employees and the passion that drove its progress was "100% Customer Satisfaction through Quality," which evolved over time to "Growth through Quality" to "Linking Buyers and Sellers in Communities and Around the World." Through a variety of measurement processes, GTE Directories gauges the effectiveness of the changes it has made and continues to make. Like Wainwright, its passion for perfection in customer service and for creating valued products has led to significant accomplishments. The company won the Baldrige Award in 1994 and has experienced increasing revenue growth in a highly competitive market. It has transformed to a $1.7 billion multi-product company, expanding beyond traditional yellow pages to embrace the information superhighway with a premium Internet shopping and directory service, SuperPages.com, as part of its quest. Its employees, who are encouraged to share the passion and are supported in their efforts to do so, take pride in their work and are among the most loyal in the business.

If conditions had not changed for GTE Directories, the organization might never have felt the need or found the opportunity to define its core passions. It might have remained profitable financially, but the quality of the relationships it formed and of the services it provided would probably never have improved. It is doubtful it would have been recognized as one of the outstanding businesses in the country, or that its employees and customers would have benefited emotionally from their involvement with the organization.

Discovery Through Intuition

Some people are born with an acute awareness of their passion. It is so strong they cannot deny it, so powerful they must follow it. For these people, and quite often for the organizations they form, passion is a product of intuition. No one needs to tell them what they feel or why. They sense the forces that energize them and make them the center of their being. There is no moment of discovery: the reality of passion simply is and always has been.

It is difficult to think of an organization as intuitive. To do so I want you to consider it as a representation of the people who form it. If a founder creates a company to support a particular passion and recruits associates who recognize and share that passion, then the organization truly embodies it. It does not discover it at a given point in its history: it is the reason for its existence.

I founded my own organization, Richard Chang Associates, Inc., as an extension of my passion for performance improvement and excellence. As a child I always strove to be the best I could, as a student, a musician, and an athlete. I was constantly looking for ways to improve my performance in all areas of my life. I knew, however, that my passion was not limited to myself. I wanted to help others achieve their potential, too. This led me to study psychology and to spend a number of years counseling individuals.

I soon became aware that counseling did not address another of my lifelong passions: entrepreneurship. I had always wanted to start my own enterprise, so I made the move to the world of business. I received a graduate degree in industrial and organizational psychology and gained valuable real-world experience and insight working for other organizations. When I felt the time was right, I made the leap to create my own. There was no question what the focus of the business would be: helping individuals and organizations improve performance. I hired people who were equally passionate about improvement and shared my enthusiasm for the work. I sought clients who appreciated what we had to offer and would truly benefit from our assistance.

There has never been a time when the core passion of my organization has been uncertain. Though our strategies and activities change from year to year based on the needs of our clients and opportunities for our own improvement, our passion—the force that drives us—remains the same.

Discovery Through Experience

Most individuals and organizations fall into the fourth and final category of discovery: discovery through experience. They discover their passions not instantaneously as lightning bolts of inspiration, not forcefully as reactions to major events, not mysteriously as the truth of their existence. They uncover them gradually as a result of day-to-day experience. The challenge in such cases is to recognize the clues that arise and actually identify the passions they reveal.

The community of Brazosport, Texas, is located fifty miles southwest of Houston on the Gulf of Mexico. It boasts approximately fifty thousand residents, and like many other communities in this country, its population includes people of a wide variety of backgrounds. When Dr. Gerald Anderson was named superintendent of the Brazosport Independent School District in 1991, there was a wide disparity in student performance between ethnic and economic groups. Test scores indicated that minority and economically disadvantaged children were achieving at levels far beneath those of their white, middle-class schoolmates.

Anderson saw this disparity, and unlike so many of his colleagues around the nation, he was not willing to merely accept it as an unfortunate reality. He realized that the lag in performance not only had consequences for the district and its perceived effectiveness but also had very real results in the lives of the students it affected. What the test scores told him was what he knew in his heart. The district was failing these children. It was not equipping them with the skills they needed to succeed in the twenty-first century. Not only were few of the children realizing their potential, many were not even beginning to tap into it.

Under Anderson's enlightened and highly capable leadership, teachers began to recognize their own dissatisfaction with the district's performance. For many there were stirrings of emotion that told them something was not right. This may not sound surprising, but many educators and businesspeople alike are willing to accept the status quo as the best that can be done. They accept problems as facts of life and resign themselves to making the best of them. Any passion they might have to change or improve things is easily buried by these perceived limitations.

Anderson was not about to do this. He understood that he and many of the teachers and faculty he led entered the field of education because they wanted to make a difference. As he told me recently, "The business we're in is one of people. We're not building cars or turning out chemicals. We're turning children into adults, and the quality of life they have is determined upon how well we do our job. And so we have to be very passionate about that because it is a moral obligation. It is a passionate thing to develop people, to make sure that you equip them with the tools so they can have a productive life."

So taking clues from his environment, namely the test scores, and from his heart, Anderson embarked on a mission to transform the district based on this core passion—teaching and empowering *all* children in its care. The results of his efforts have been phenomenal. Between 1991 and 1998, the proportion of economically disadvantaged students in the Brazosport district that passed the Texas Assessment of Academic Skills in reading rose from 60 percent to 91 percent; in math from 54 percent to 93 percent; and in writing from 57 percent to 90 percent. The numbers for minority groups are equally impressive. The proportion of Hispanic and African American students passing the tests increased by at least 30 percentage points in each area, with no group boasting anything less than a 90 percent pass rate in any area. Because the district's focus is all students, performance of nonminority students also improved markedly.

The numbers are not just data. They are a reflection of the shared passion of the associates of Brazosport Independent School District, a passion that emerged because Gerald Anderson and others were willing to listen to their hearts. It took shape gradually as they investigated and learned from their environment, but quickly became the center of the organization's efforts and the driving force behind its progress.

Steps to Discovery

If the organization has lost sight of its passions, or has never truly discovered them, there is much it can do to uncover them. The process should begin with leaders. They are responsible for the organization's direction and possess the power to implement organization-wide changes. Though passion can grow within the organization from any source and at any level, the most forceful and effective change emanates from leadership.

Passion Review

Types of Discovery
- *Discovery by epiphany.* A single pivotal experience makes leaders or associates suddenly and intensely aware of an underlying passion.
- *Discovery through change.* A major change such as the emergence of a competitor, the death of a leader, or a major development in technology leads to a realization of a passion.
- *Discovery through intuition.* A passion simply makes itself felt, naturally and undeniably.
- *Discovery through experience.* Gradual awareness of passion develops through day-to-day operations and experiences.

If you are not a key leader in your organization or are not in a position to initiate the discovery process on behalf of the entire group, consider the steps that follow from a personal perspective. When I mention leadership, consider yourself. When I discuss the organization, insert your job within the organization. This will help you to uncover your own passions regarding the organization and your role within it.

The Leadership Retreat

To begin the process of discovery, the key leaders in the organization must take a step back from the day-to-day frenzy of the business and seek a fresh perspective. They must be able to shut out the noise and confusion of everyday operations and find the peace necessary to reflect. Though there is a slight chance this could be accomplished at a one-day offsite in the conference room of a nearby hotel, I suggest an actual retreat to a location that is as far removed in atmosphere as it is in distance. The retreat is not to be a traditional business meeting, after all, but an awakening, and where would you rather awaken—in the mountains, at the beach, or at the downtown convention center?

In choosing a location, leaders should realize that the most important factor to the retreat's success is perspective. It is critical to discovery because it eliminates the trivialities and perceptions that distract us from recognizing passion in the first place. Given distance, matters of seemingly great urgency become insignificant. Issues that dominate thinking and absorb energy on the job seem inconsequential. And goals that seem critical to success recede in importance.

I find that the most successful locations are those that naturally inspire emotion. Settings of exceptional beauty or serenity such as secluded mountaintops and remote islands are particularly effective in arousing thoughts and feelings we normally suppress. Once unleashed, these ideas and emotions help us to view reality through new eyes. We appreciate the underappreciated, see the good in the bad, and recognize possibilities we never imagined.

Despite leaders' fears, chances are that when they return, nothing will have changed in their absence. No crises will have erupted, no new competitors will have popped up, the building will still be standing. What will have changed are the leaders themselves. They will have opened their hearts to potential passions and begun seeing the organization in a new light.

Creating the Passion Profile

Once they have escaped the exigencies of the real world and are safely ensconced, free of distraction and conflict, in a secluded setting, the leaders' first task is to relax. The second is to create a Passion Profile of the organization. The profile is a document aimed at revealing any and all potential core passions of the organization. It is not a final declaration of such passions, only a starting point for further inquiry.

Drafting the profile requires leaders to look to many sources for passion clues. They must look inside themselves both as individuals and as a group. They must consider associate and customer concerns, and evaluate the organization's past, present, and future. All this may seem like a lot of work, but the profile that results is invaluable. It is a window into the heart of the organization and a basis for passion-driven change.

I will describe each of the elements of the Passion Profile here in detail. To see what the profile itself looks like, take a look at the worksheet at the end of the chapter.

Understanding Content- and Context-Based Passion

Before leaders begin listing potential passions, they need to understand the two basic types of passion: content- and context-based. I use these terms because people often get confused when pinpointing their passion sources. *Content-based passion* centers on a highly specialized activity, such as a particular sport or art form. If I have a passion for baseball, then the reason I participate in the sport—either as a spectator or a player—is my love of the game. I am not drawn to it because I like competition or large crowds. I could find either of those things at a football game or a basketball game. I am excited by baseball because it is what it is, nothing less and nothing more.

Now picture an alternate scenario. I love attending baseball games and watching them on TV, but I also love playing tennis and going to boxing matches. My passion is not for any particular sport, but for the more general theme of competition. My passion is *context-based:* it is contingent not on a specific activity but on a certain characteristic that is shared by a number of activities.

To clarify the difference between content- and context-based passion, let's return to the example offered by Mind-Spring and EarthLink. Prior to their merger, both were passion-driven organizations involved in the same business. Though they shared a passion for customer service, the core passions that defined them differed. EarthLink's passion was content-based. It was a passion for the Internet, for the technology behind it, and for the possibilities it offers. Mind-Spring's passion was for building a better business, regardless of the field. It was context-based. The organization could have been devoted to the Internet, sporting goods, or firewood, and the underlying passion would be the same.

The distinction between the two can be critical to an organization's success. If leaders mistakenly identify a business's core passion as content-driven and cling too rigidly to a specific item or idea, they might miss critical opportunities for growth and expansion into other areas. If, on the other hand, they assume context is what matters but content drives the business, then efforts to branch out or move away from content can prove destructive.

Passion Review

Content-based passions center on a highly specialized topic, such as a particular sport or art form. *Context-based* passions center on a theme that can apply to one or more activities or topics, such as competition or improvement.

Leaders' Individual Passions

To begin defining the organization's Passion Profile, leaders must first look within themselves for answers: they must identify their personal passions. This is important for many reasons. First, leaders who are not in touch with their individual passions cannot encourage and develop shared passions within a group. Second, since leadership decides what the organization does and how it does it, each individual's passions have a significant impact on how these decisions are made. Third, leaders are often drawn to organizations because they in some way reflect their passions. By recognizing this connection, they can identify ways that their personal passions can be employed in moving the organization forward.

This exercise may be simple for some but difficult for others. If leaders are out of touch with their passions, they will not be able to list them. In this case they need to use the retreat as an opportunity for personal discovery. This is crucial because they cannot create a passion-driven organization without calling their own passion into play.

Every now and then, after awakening to their passions, leaders may find that these passions simply do not fit into the context of the organization, regardless of how it might change in the future. In such a case they have probably already sensed something is wrong. They might have been uncomfortable or unhappy in their position, but at the same time too afraid or cautious to make a change. My advice in such a situation echoes my warning to the organization: *If you are not passionate about an organization or a job, you have no business being in it.*

I am not the only one who has noted that individual passion is a necessity in leaders. Authors Thomas J. Neff and James N. Citrin recognized this phenomenon in their book *Lessons from the Top: The Search for America's Best Business Leaders.* Regarding the fifty top executives, Neff said, "What was clear with everyone we sat down with was that they were passionate about what they were doing. They loved to talk about it. . . . When the passion gives way, that's when you know it's time for that person to move on" (quoted in "In Search of Leadership," 1999, p. 172).

Think for a moment about the power executives hold. Though in most large companies their decisions are subject to support or criticism from a board of directors, their individual views and desires can set the tenor of the organization. A CEO who is passionate about technology can chart an entirely different course for a business from the one chosen by a CEO who is passionate about people. And when leaders' passion is an active force in their leadership, the benefits for the organization are limitless.

This is why it is imperative that leaders identify their own core passions before moving forward to identify those of the organization. While they cannot decree them to be one in the same, they can look for synergies between the two. In the case that there is no common ground, then they can as Neff and Citrin noted, move on.

Leaders' Shared Passions

Assuming most leaders will find resonance between their personal passions and the organization, the next step is to compile a list of shared passions. The reason for this is obvious: while a single leader can carve a path for the organization, no one can follow such a path successfully on their own. They need the support and enthusiasm of fellow leaders. The core passion of the organization should of necessity reflect the passions not just of one key figure, but of the entire group. While the lists of individual passions will reveal the personalities and interests leaders bring to the group, the shared list will identify the sources of their collective strength and energy.

Creating this list is not as simple as looking for overlap between the individual ones. Though doing so is a start, it is more important for the leaders to identify the things about the organization that are moving and meaningful to them *as a group*. What passions do they share about the business? What inspires them in their professional roles? What are they proud of in the organization? What draws them to it? What keeps them there? What do they wish were better?

Many of the items that appear on this list might not be an official part of company culture but have evolved informally over the years. Some might be hopes rather than realities. Others might have been lost in the wake of change. Whatever the case, because they are common to the group, they are significant. Unless leaders are completely out of touch with the heart of the organization—meaning it exists despite them rather than as a result of them—the passions they share will be a central force in guiding its future.

Associate and Customer Passions

Another critical step in creating the Passion Profile is considering the passions of both associates and customers. Why do they seek out the organization? What, if anything, excites them about it? Do they share common characteristics? Leaders must remember that these are the people who keep the business running, who create and consume its products and services, and who provide the resources necessary for its future survival. Though they may not carry official responsibility for setting policy or defining strategy, they often do so by virtue of their importance to the organization.

If employees are passionate about a particular product, they might lobby to keep it alive. If it is eliminated, their initiative may wane and their performance may deteriorate. If customers are passionate about a program, they will most certainly be disappointed if it is removed. They may demand it be reinstated or threaten to take their business elsewhere. If, however, the new program builds on the same elements that aroused their passion in the first place, their support might be stronger than it was before; this in turn might lead to the development of other similar programs.

If leaders are sensitive to cues such as these, then they will understand the passions that drive the organization from the grassroots level. These passions are not hypothetical or merely possible: they exist. Arrogant leadership may choose to ignore or dismiss them, but smart leaders understand them to be signs of success and pointers to future possibilities.

Historical Passions

Because many organizations are founded on passion, leaders should also look to the past when creating the Passion Profile. They need to answer questions such as these: What passions have played a part in the history of the business? What motivated the original owners to create it? What did they seek to accomplish, and why? Did the organization's focus or inspiration change along the way? Why?

If the business has strayed from its roots, leaders may be surprised to learn that passion once defined it or at least drove its progress. They may be even more surprised to uncover the reasons that passion was lost or mismanaged along the way. Often a single change in strategy or response to market forces can set the organization off track and turn it away from its core passions. Made in succession such decisions can lead the organization so far from its passions that they no longer seem relevant or recognizable.

In such cases listing previous passions may require research: interviews with founders or early leaders, review of internal documents from the company archives, examination of old advertisements and publicity campaigns, anything that might highlight where the energy came from in those early days.

Some people feel that passion by definition is about the future, that it has no relevance to the past. They are sorely mistaken. Passions do not fizzle or become outdated. They may fade from view because they are ignored or neglected, but they remain nonetheless.

A company founded at the turn of the century based on a passion for entertainment can preserve that passion over the decades whether it is involved in carnivals, movie theaters, or cyberarcades. If somehow the business shifted direction and is now devoted to food service, it may come as no surprise that the original energy and enthusiasm have disappeared. What may be surprising, however, is that they probably remain, albeit in latent form. Perhaps employees or customers are attracted to the mythology of the early company. Maybe leaders are drawn in by the tradition of this early spirit or a hope that it still exists. Or perhaps some of those who shared that passion are still around, ready to bring it back to life if given the opportunity.

Core Competencies

Just as the past is important in pointing the way to the future, so is the present. An integral part of the Passion Profile is an examination of the organization's present strengths. Core competencies are those areas in which the organization has established proficiency, or in simpler terms, what it's good at. Leaders need to evaluate their core competencies—and, more important, the areas in which the organization excels to reveal potential passion sources.

As I have emphasized many times already, passion drives performance. Any area of unusual strength or superior performance suggests that passion is at work. If leaders have not already done so, they must identify the passions underlying these achievements so as to evaluate how they may be built upon in the future.

Leaders should consider core competencies on a more pragmatic level. They should not be equated with passion for one simple reason: you do not have to love something to be good at it. They do, however, indicate basic skills that can be employed in pursuing passion-driven growth.

Future Opportunities

Whether leaders are conscious of passion or not, they must constantly be focused on the future. To remain competitive in today's marketplace companies must constantly innovate, if not in technological terms then in their approaches to customer service and product development. As leaders build the Passion Profile for the organization, they should look to the future for signs of potential passions.

Given the situation today, what possibilities excite them about tomorrow? Where do they see opportunities for tapping into current passion sources or discovering new ones? Where do they see the most significant opportunities for business development and growth?

Their answers to these questions are just as revealing as those they provided in other areas of the profile. Leaders' hopes and visions for the future necessarily encompass passion. Out of caution or fear they may settle for less than they should, but their highest aspirations for the organization's progress reflect the passions they wish it to embody.

Passion Review

Factors to consider in creating the organization's
Passion Profile:

Leaders' Personal Passions   Historical Passions
Leaders' Shared Passions   Core Competencies
Associate and Customer Passions   Future Opportunities

Putting It All Together:
Identifying the Organization's Core Passions

Once the lists in the worksheet at the end of the chapter are
compiled, leaders need to sit down, think, and—more important—feel. As they consider everything that has been listed,
they must decide which few key elements really define the
spirit they want the organization to exude. What are the factors that must absolutely remain? Which will define the heart
of the business as it is now or as they hope it to be in the
future? What items have the potential to powerfully and consistently motivate associates, or already do?

Though many of the passions listed can function simultaneously in the organization, there must be a few that stand out.
There must be two or three that will guide its efforts as times
and circumstances change: these are the core passions. They are
the nonnegotiables of the organization. They cannot and will
not be compromised. All decisions that are made and actions
that are taken will support them. They will not be forsaken or

forgotten for the sake of pragmatism or prudence. They will remain the driving and defining force behind the business.

Again, I must emphasize that the core passions defined at this early stage are not written in stone. They may change as leaders become more familiar with passion and are more capable of identifying it. If the organization is "devoid of feeling," the Passion Profile might be more an exercise in guesswork than certainty or intuition. As leaders strive to take a heart-first approach, they will become more sensitive to the emotional side of the organization. They will begin to recognize passion without having to search for it. Subsequently, they might realize they were mistaken in their initial attempts and identify new core passions.

For those organizations already on the heart-first track, the core passions that emerge from the Passion Profile may seem obvious. Perhaps they are, but that is irrelevant. The important point is that they now have been overtly identified, whereas before they were only hinted at or assumed to exist. Core passions can become the platform for the organization only if they are clearly articulated and appreciated, and leaders have done both.

Those who have lingered in passion limbo, or somewhere between the extremes of the Passion Scale, have probably produced a fairly accurate picture of their organizations' passions. Though the profile may be subject to future revision, chances are it is a solid starting point for aligning the business with its passion.

Whatever the case, whatever the organization's passion history, leaders are now prepared to move forward, as are associates who have embarked on their discovery at a personal level. They are ready to take the core passions they have identified and build on them. Their next step will be to clarify the purpose that these passions will serve, so they can begin using them not only to revitalize the organization or their individual jobs but also to achieve specific goals.

Actions for Associates

You may not be in a position to decide the fate and future direction of your organization, but you can determine what inspires you about it. This is your personal window into the heart of the organization. Once you have identified your passions surrounding the organization, you can share them with leaders. If enough associates do so, the chance that leaders will awaken to these passions increases exponentially. You cannot force them to listen, but you can make sure they know where you—an impassioned associate—stand.

PASSION PLAN WORKSHEET #2

Step Two: Discover Core Passions	How
A. The Key Focus of the Organization's Passion Profile Includes:	What passions have been discovered that the organization could build upon? • Discovery by epiphany • Discovery through change • Discovery through intuition • Discovery through experience Note: Remember to also consider several critical questions about the organization when trying to discover its core passions, including: • Where is the organization today? • Where does the organization want to be tomorrow? • What regrets haunt the organization?
B. Passions the Organization Could Build Upon: 1. Leaders' Personal Passions . . . 2. Leaders' Shared Passions . . .	Define and clarify the important focuses and the priorities for each of the following: • Leaders' personal passions • Leaders' shared passions

Passion Plan Worksheet #2 (cont.)

3. Associate and Customer Passions . . .

4. Organization's Historical Passions . . .

5. Core Competencies . . .

6. Future Opportunities . . .

- Associate and customer passions
- Organization's historical passions
- Core competencies
- Future opportunities

C. **Potential Passion "Taste Tests" and Ways to Taste:**

1.

2.

3.

Identify potential passions that the organization wants to newly instill or build back in its culture using a "taste test" approach. In addition, list some potential ways to carry out a "taste test." Remember:

- These are passions that you want to begin building into the organization on its own terms.
- Find nonthreatening ways to allow the organization to experience the passions.

Passionism...

"Passion is part of you; purpose is something you create."

CHAPTER 5

Step Three: Clarify Purpose

Channeling the Organization's Passion Toward a Specific Goal

The secret to success is constancy of purpose.
—BENJAMIN DISRAELI

Identifying the organization's core passions can be a liberating feat. Discovering the sources of its potential and the keys to its future is exciting and inspiring. Once they have been through Step Two, leaders and associates often feel that there is nothing the organization cannot accomplish. While their enthusiasm is justified, there is much more that needs to be done before they can truly seize their passions and run with them.

The immediate task is to decide where the core passions will lead the organization. Everyone understands that they can unleash enthusiasm and energy, but how will that energy be used? What end will passion serve? What will its purpose be? Will it make the world a better place? Will it enrich employees' lives? Fill investors' wallets? Set higher technological standards?

Create a new industry? The possibilities are infinite, and with passion at work, none is impossible.

But to be truly effective, passion must be managed. It must be channeled. Those using it must clarify the specific results they hope to achieve. If they fail to do so, passion may flourish—but at the expense of the organization. Associates can follow it in opposing directions or use it to justify irrational or counterproductive actions. Customers can misinterpret it and leaders can abuse it. To avoid such failures, the organization must take Step Three and establish a clear sense of purpose that will guide the way it uses its passions. Associates seeking change at the personal level should take the same measures to determine how they will use their own passions within the scope of their role in the organization.

How Purpose Works

Many people are taken aback when I discuss *passion management*. They consider the term an oxymoron. They mistakenly believe that a force as powerful and spontaneous as passion cannot be controlled. They believe that assigning it a specific role necessarily constrains it. I argue the opposite. Think of passion as a raging river. What benefit do we derive from it if it flows unchecked? Its energy is dispersed erratically in the form of floods, currents, and whirlpools. But if we channel the powerful waters using dams and levies, we harness its energy. We gain the ability not only to control its flow but also to direct its course.

I use this example not to anger environmentalists, only to illustrate a point: passion can be channeled to bring about very specific results. Its energy can be directed to maximize its potential rather than waste it. To help you understand the relationship between passion and purpose, consider the example of Ben & Jerry's.

Most people in the United States recognize the name. It conjures images of hippies in tie-dye shirts and funky ice creams with names such as Wavy Gravy, Chubby Hubby, and Cherry Garcia. The story of how two unassuming, everyday fellows, Ben Cohen and Jerry Greenfield, turned a single ice cream shop into a wildly successful worldwide operation provides a valuable lesson in passion management.

Finding themselves at a crossroads in their lives, longtime friends Ben and Jerry decided to start a business. The only question was what kind. Neither had ever held a job that translated into a viable start-up operation, so they looked to their hearts (and their stomachs) for an answer. They explain in their book *Ben & Jerry's Double-Dip,* "Since eating was our greatest passion, it seemed logical to start a restaurant business" (Cohen and Greenfield, 1997, p. 15). The reason they chose ice cream was even simpler: ice cream makers and freezers were cheaper than bagel-making equipment.

Ben and Jerry's early actions were fueled by a variety of passions beyond the one they professed for food. First, they were driven by a desire to build something of their own. Second, there was no question in their minds that creating a business gave them a unique opportunity to give back to the community, something they had both aspired to do in their previous work. Money, although a necessity, was never a passion. Their short-term objective was to earn a living, but they set their goals no higher than $20,000 in annual salary.

Because they were passionate about the business, the struggles they encountered the first few years did not daunt them. They remember that despite serious financial and operational challenges, "We were having a great time. We were totally engaged in what we were doing. It was clear people loved our ice cream, and that felt really good" (Cohen and Greenfield, 1997, p. 18). What also made them feel good was the fulfillment of their desire to contribute to the community. Before they ever turned a profit, they found reasons to give away ice cream. No matter how foolish others thought their actions, they knew in their hearts that this was one of the reasons they were in business; it was one of their core passions.

As the years passed and their business grew, Ben and Jerry realized that their passion for giving back could be more than just a passion. It could actually define the business. They were passionate about their ice cream, but more passionate about what the profits it generated could do for individuals and communities. They prided themselves on producing a high-quality product, but derived greater pleasure from enlisting social underdogs to help them do it.

Faced with the decision of selling out or holding on, Ben saw that out of this passion stemmed an even greater purpose: making the business a force for progressive social change. Subsequently, Ben and Jerry and the executives they have hired over the years to lead the now $230 million per year business have dedicated themselves to values-led business, or as current CEO Perry Odak terms it, the practice of "caring capitalism." Everything that the organization does—every decision it makes, every partnership it forms, every flavor it develops, every package it prints—is fueled by the passion to give back and guided by this purpose.

Ben & Jerry's has shocked much of the business world with its success. Many doubted that such a business could survive, much less flourish. After all, the company contributes 7.5 percent of its annual profits to charity; publishes an annual social and environmental performance assessment; spends hundreds of thousands of extra dollars on environmentally conscious packaging; gives away millions of free ice cream cones every year; and sells its products only in countries where its purpose can be fulfilled. None of these seem like profit-generating practices.

Not surprisingly to me, or to anyone who is guided by the heart, Ben & Jerry's has succeeded because of and not despite its passion. And because this passion has been so clearly directed by purpose, it has bred very specific results. Ben and Jerry write, "Unlike most commercial transactions, buying a product from a company you believe in transcends the purchase. It touches your soul. Our customers don't like just our ice cream—they like what our company stands for. They like how doing business with us makes them feel. . . . The more we actualize our commitment to social change through our business activities, the more loyal customers we attract and the more profitable we become" (Cohen and Greenfield, 1997, p. 31).

Ben & Jerry's could have taken many paths in pursuing its passion. It could have proclaimed a worldwide mission to bring low-cost ice cream to the masses. This might have prompted it to use the cheapest ingredients instead of more expensive, environmentally and socially beneficial ones, such as sustainably harvested rain-forest nuts from Brazil, coffee beans from a small cooperative of Mexican peasant farmers, and brownies from a bakery that employs economically disenfranchised workers. To best serve this purpose, the organization might have gone with the cheapest suppliers rather than those owned by minorities and those aligned with the company's values.

Another alternative could have been to give back simply by donating a higher percentage of profits to charity. Many businesses limit their commitment to social causes to a check written at the end of the year. Their awareness and their aggressiveness end when the check is dropped in the mail. Though their motives are questionable, they are still "giving back." By defining its purpose, Ben & Jerry's proved itself different. The underwriters of the company's national public stock offering threatened to abandon the deal if the business contributed any more than 7.5 percent of its profits annually (most companies average about 1.5 percent). Ben and Jerry figured they could live with that if they were focused on giving back in other ways. Their purpose was greater than cash gifts (Cohen and Greenfield, 1997, p. 101).

They also could have decided that creating world-class, super premium ice cream was a sufficient way of giving back. After all, ice cream stirs fond feelings and makes happy bellies. Providing people with a high-quality, feel-good product could have been enough. But it wasn't. Because ice cream is the economic engine that drives the company's ability to pursue its social mission, producing a consistently superior product is as important an objective.

Big Purpose

The purpose that the leaders of Ben & Jerry's defined has determined the nature of its efforts in significant and far-reaching ways. It has directed the way the organization follows its core passions and distinguishes its objectives. It demonstrates the importance of what I call "Big Purpose."

Big Purpose is the organization's overarching sense of mission. It is the rationale for its activities, its justification for being. As I will discuss later in the chapter, the organization possesses many purposes in a variety of areas, but Big Purpose underlies everything else. Without it, nothing else matters.

Like passion, Big Purpose stems from the heart. In fact, the two are closely if not inextricably linked. They work in tandem. To clarify, consider the case of Southwest Airlines. Perhaps one of the most revered and well-documented companies in the world, Southwest embodies passion. In fact, it is driven by many passions, including fun, creativity, customer service, and profitability. But there is one core passion that from the organization's inception drove its founders and shaped its Big Purpose: freedom.

In 1966 San Antonio businessman Rollin King and banker John Parker approached lawyer Herb Kelleher about forming a new intrastate airline. At a time when most air travelers were either wealthy or businesspeople, travel between the major cities in Texas was both inconvenient and expensive. Though Kelleher anticipated a major fight from the national airlines, he jumped on board. He thought the idea, as crazy as it seemed, might just work.

Sure enough, as soon as the Texas Aeronautics Commission approved Southwest's application to fly, its competitors filed a restraining order, preventing the commission from issuing the necessary certificate. And this was just the first in a long line of attacks. It took more than four years, a series of lawsuits, and a trip to the Texas Supreme Court for Southwest to get a single plane off the ground.

Things didn't get much easier once the tiny airline was up and running. Its competitors continued to bombard it with lawsuits, marketing blitzes, and underhanded tactics, apparently prepared to stop at nothing to destroy the new competitor. In 1975, the federal government indicted Braniff and Texas International for conspiring to put Southwest out of business. They quietly pleaded no contest, paid a fine, and walked away.

What were the other airlines so afraid of? Southwest was an upstart with tremendous odds stacked against it. But it threatened to rock the very foundations of the airline industry by committing what amounted to heresy: lowering fares. Less passionate folk might have failed, but Kelleher and his associates were driven by what they call a "warrior spirit." Besieged by giants, they immediately found themselves in the role of the underdog. Forced to fight daily for their survival, they developed a passion for freedom—from harassment by competitors and from practices that were unfair to consumers.

This passion translated into a mission. Southwest would not only make the business commuter's travel easier and save corporate customers some money, it would make air travel affordable and accessible to everyone. It would bring freedom to the skies. This was a bold desire in a time when only one in four Americans had ever flown. Today, however, this number has risen to three out of every four, and it is no stretch to claim that Southwest is responsible for the change.

Whenever Southwest enters a market it creates what the company calls the Southwest effect. Rather than taking a piece of the existing market, it generates a bigger one. People who normally would drive or take the bus between destinations fly instead. Those who might not have left at all have a convenient and affordable means of vacationing or visiting friends and relatives. And certainly a number who were already flying exercise their freedom to save time and money by switching to Southwest.

Employees defend their purpose zealously. They subscribe to the slogan, "It's not a job, it's a crusade." Signs of their mission are evident everywhere: a company logo reads: *Southwest Airlines: A Symbol of Freedom;* employees and non-employees alike are recognized with Freedom Fighter awards; and corporate newsletters proclaim the company's efforts to expand its "freedom movement." A recent edition of *LUVLines* (the employee newsletter) summed up the company's purpose in an article headed, "East Coast Freedom Revolution Underway." It began, "In 1998, 171 communities asked Southwest for something no other airline could offer them: FREEDOM . . . from high fares, from lackluster service, from price-gouging airlines."

The passion for freedom and the commitment to providing it to customers has guided Southwest's efforts for the last thirty years. Employees realize that if the company were to ground its fleet tomorrow, competitors would hike their fares immediately, and millions would lose their freedom to fly. The organization's Big Purpose is to maintain this freedom for its customers: it is the basis of its business. Without it Southwest would lose the ability to exercise its own freedom as an innovator, or as Southwest employees like to call it, a "color outside the lines" company.

Both Southwest and Ben & Jerry's have defined rather awe-inspiring Big Purposes. This should not intimidate leaders of smaller organizations that have more humble aspirations. A company does not have to transform an industry or create a new form of business in order to be important. What matters is that it has direction, that associates know why they are involved and what their efforts are intended to achieve. If they have a clear vision of Big Purpose and share the passion that underlies it, they will be prepared to give their all in working toward it.

Your organization's Big Purpose might already be evident, even if it has not been overtly stated. It might be as lofty as saving lives or as simple as having fun, which, by the way, should not be discounted as a valid aim. Some organizations are started with the purpose of making money, but usually there is much more to it than that. Founders may seek above all to create a company that endures or that produces consistently innovative products. Their greatest desire might be to bring happiness to customers or opportunities for development to employees.

Those clarifying the organization's Big Purpose need to understand only two key points. The first is that—as the name implies—Big Purpose is *big*. It is not a temporary objective or a fleeting concern. It is a lasting desire. It is bigger than the present, something that looms in the future and requires constant effort to achieve. It is not a finite goal or a stopping point, it is a starting point for growth.

The second point to remember is that Big Purpose is necessarily an extension of passion. It is emotion-driven, not calculated or contrived. Our goals are not meaningful if they do not stem from the heart. If we are not excited about them, there is little chance we will have the commitment or energy necessary to achieve them. Southwest Airlines could not have endured its struggles if it had not been passionate about its commitment to bringing freedom to the skies. Ben & Jerry's could not have leapt the hurdles to creating a values-led, socially committed company if it had not been passionate about giving back to the community. Simply stated, passion informs Big Purpose and is the means of working toward it.

Passion Review

Big Purpose is the organization's overarching sense of mission. It is the rationale for its activities and its justification for being.

Mission and Vision

There is a chance that your organization's Big Purpose has already been expressed in the form of a vision or mission statement. Both are valid concepts and often reflect the passions and purpose of the organizations professing them. You should be careful, however, not to trust in such statements blindly. Just because something has been put onto paper does not mean it is accurate. Many organizations are so confused by what the terms mean that the statements they produce are nothing more than an exercise in guesswork, garbled expressions of what leaders think they should be rather than reflections of reality. Some organizations feel compelled to create vision and mission statements because consultants tell them they should or because everyone else has. In such cases, they often fail to grasp their intent. Instead of emotion-charged statements of direction they end up with hollow phrases that do not reflect the spirit of the organization. Many statements use the right format and contain the right terms but hang on the wall collecting dust because there is nothing behind them.

The terms *vision* and *mission* both imply a sense of something greater. They hint that there is more to progress than just forging ahead. There is commitment, there is energy, and there is passion. Do not spend time worrying about semantics. For the heart-first organization there is no distinction between vision or mission or goals. Instead, there is passion, and passion translates into Big Purpose, pure and simple. You start with passion and then decide where you want it to lead you. End of story.

Key Profit Areas

In fulfilling its Big Purpose, Southwest is inspired to do the absolute best it can not only to stay in business but also to excel. This includes keeping costs low, treating all customers (a term used for both employees and passengers) with love and respect, and making things fun. Each of these objectives is a passion for the organization and contributes to upholding the Big Purpose.

The same is true of Ben & Jerry's. While its Big Purpose is becoming a force for social change, it has to consider many other objectives in making this possible. It must, like all sustainable businesses, turn a profit. To accomplish this, it must produce ice cream that consumers want to buy. This means ensuring quality and developing desirable flavors. Both in turn require skill from employees and safety from facilities. The list of concerns goes on and on, but all point back to one end—Big Purpose.

These examples highlight the fact that working toward Big Purpose involves many smaller, more specific and immediate purposes. Leaders cannot simply build passion in the organization and then expect Big Purpose to materialize. In envisioning the organization's future, they must necessarily consider its financial status; the nature of its relationships with employees, partners, and customers; its professional contributions; and its role as a member of society. These I call "key profit areas." Each is an essential element of the organization and has the potential to support or detract from Big Purpose.

To help you begin to see the organization's activities in this light—as a complex of purposes that form one Big Purpose—here are eight key profit areas and examples of the purpose an organization might seek in each.

Financial. All for-profit organizations are driven by a need to make money. After all, without profits, there is no business. Even nonprofit organizations must keep a close eye on the bottom line, as they are accountable for how effectively their dollars are used. Because some degree of financial stability is essential to every organization, leaders must identify their goals in this area. At this stage they do not need to target specific numbers or percentages, but they should have a general idea of what they hope to achieve. They might define success as slow but consistent growth, rapidly increasing profit margins, or anything better than breaking even. The range of possibilities is wide, because contrary to what many may think, not all companies are motivated by a desire to make the most money possible!

Interpersonal. Organizations do not exist without people. They are a product of relationships between leaders, associates, partners, and customers. The people involved judge the success of the organization largely on the quality of these relationships. Strong bonds increase loyalty, build business, and promote growth, while weak ones undermine the foundations of the group. Leaders must define what constitutes success in terms of these relationships.

Internal (Employees). Many organizations are coming to the realization that employees are their most valuable asset. They possess the talent, energy, and initiative to bring about all types of Profit. To attract and retain employees, organizations are emphasizing qualities such as freedom, flexibility, and trust. They understand that an investment in associates is an investment in the future of the organization. As a result, many define purpose in this area as creating a fulfilled, productive workforce. It could also entail improving employees' lives through means such as education, financial benefits, and professional opportunities.

External (Customers and Partners). The same organizations that are devoted to improving internal relationships are often focused on strengthening external relationships as well. Customer service has become an obsession for many, as they recognize the connection between satisfied customers and business growth. With more options than ever, consumers no longer have to accept shoddy products or rude service. As a result, many organizations have begun to evaluate their success in terms of customer satisfaction. Purpose in such cases might be defined as exceeding expectations, meeting every need every time, or building permanent rather than transactional relationships.

Partners, vendors, distributors, retailers, and contractors also influence the organization. Leaders must evaluate the importance of these relationships and decide what they hope to gain from them. Do they wish only to fulfill contractual obligations on an as-needed basis in order to keep things running smoothly, or do they hope for more? Perhaps their purpose is to create alliances that will expand their opportunities or to build trust between businesses.

Professional. Every organization must consider what it hopes to achieve in its field. Southwest defines itself as a customer service organization that happens to be an airline, but it still faces airline-related issues. It cannot ignore the idea that it has planes to maintain and pilots to train. Likewise Ben & Jerry's is part of the frozen confection industry. It must decide what contributions it will make that are specific to ice cream. Purposes leaders might define in this area include being recognized as best in field, winning industry awards, or improving industry technology and processes.

Spiritual. This might seem an odd area to consider, but there is a spiritual element to organizations. Many are simply oblivious to it. Most of the groups profiled in this book have a deep sense of conviction about their efforts. They believe their actions have ramifications beyond financial and professional levels and that their businesses can have a lasting impact on the lives of individuals and the workings of society. They have invested much more than time and money in their work and seek a greater, intangible reward. This is the spiritual dimension of business. As an example, organizations might seek to inspire customers or enhance associates' personal awareness.

Civic. Because organizations are part of the communities they inhabit, they should evaluate the purpose and level of their involvement in them. Will they pay their taxes and call it good or try to make more significant contributions? Most passion-driven organizations recognize that the rewards of active participation in the community far outweigh the costs. Purpose in this area could include improving quality of life, supporting political causes, or providing necessary services.

Humanitarian. Contributions don't stop at the local level. They extend to include states, nations, and even humankind. Any organization that intends to last needs to decide what it will contribute to society, or in the words of Ben and Jerry, what it will give back. Will it donate a percentage of profits to charities? Will it participate in humanitarian organizations? Will it create its own programs to improve the lives of others? Its purpose in this area might be to do none of the above, only to benefit society by its existence. There is a greater probabili-

Passion Review

Key Profit Areas are the many smaller, more specific and immediate purposes that should support an organization's Big Purpose. They include the following:

Financial

Interpersonal

Internal (employees)

External (customers and partners)

Professional

Spiritual

Civic

Humanitarian

ty that it will be something more, but what exactly must be clear.

The goals the organization defines in each of these key profit areas function together to bring purpose down from the realm of idealism into the world of day-to-day reality. They require leaders to implement initiatives, programs, and policies that support Big Purpose and give associates something more tangible to grasp in performing their jobs.

Aligning Purpose

The challenge in working to achieve results in each of the key profit areas is remaining focused on Big Purpose. Organizations that are not careful in this regard find themselves working to contrary ends. There must be consistency between purposes. For example, Ben & Jerry's would be defeating its Big Purpose if it did not strive to build alliances with partners that supported its efforts, if not in action then at least in spirit. Southwest would lose credibility in the eyes of its employees if it sang a song of freedom, but enforced authoritarian policies that denied them their own.

This admonition may seem obvious, but many organizations that are committed to a passion-inspired Big Purpose make just such mistakes. They lose sight of the big picture in the face of challenges and make decisions grounded in fear or logic. Even Ben & Jerry's, an exemplar of consistency to purpose, has strayed. When the company first began international operations, leaders did not consider the relevance of the organization's purpose. According to CEO Odak, "There was no social mission. We were just selling product." Despite the lure of increased revenue, leaders quickly revised their plans, pulling out of some countries and adjusting their practices in others. Odak explains, "We decided we were not just going to sell ice cream into these marketplaces and bring our profits back to the United States. We knew we needed to return to those communities and stand for something good as part of doing business with them."

To prevent such mistakes, members of the organization need to evaluate not only what their objectives are in each area, but also the ways in which the organization's core passions can serve these purposes. Remember—passion will enable the organization to fulfill its purposes and to reach its Profit.

This is where the thinking element of the Passion Plan at Work comes into play. Leaders need to be smart; they need to use their heads. They need to look for possibilities rather than limitations, opportunities rather than obstacles. Above all, they need to make sure that Big Purpose remains preeminent.

Consider the following example. A bank has a core passion for family, for creating feelings of support and connectedness between associates in the organization. Its Big Purpose is to make people's lives easier by providing necessary and valuable financial services. How do the two relate to one another? Will this core passion fuel the Big Purpose, or will it just help employees feel at home while on the job? I have seen organizations that do an excellent job at building camaraderie among associates, but often one of two things happens. Employees feel so secure that they either extend this sense of security to customers through friendliness and superior service or close them out by assuming an almost elitist attitude. Clearly, the bank is not going to make people's lives easier, and there will be significantly less value to its service, if its employees are difficult to deal with. On the contrary, if they project the family feeling to customers, there will be inherent value to the service it is providing and it will be one step closer to achieving its Big Purpose.

Leaders could assume the two are already connected, but they would be foolish to do so. They could also fail to see the possible connection and lose a powerful resource. What they must do instead is identify the potential relationship and then look for means to ensure that one serves the other. Theoretically, increased security should translate into increased satisfaction, which should in turn lead to increased performance. To guarantee this happens, the bank's leaders could build on their existing accomplishment in a number of ways: they could create employee training programs, make employees directly accountable for customer satisfaction, or heighten their awareness by casting them in customer roles.

Though I have mentioned some options, the specific steps leaders decide to take are not what matters at this point. The important thing is that they establish the possible connections between passion and purpose. For any passion-based action they take to be effective, it must serve the organization's purposes. This alignment is critical and must be envisioned before changes are made.

To begin this process, leaders should use the worksheet at the end of the chapter. Associates can use the same worksheet to identify the purpose of the passions they bring to their positions.

Actions for Associates

If your organization has not clearly defined its Big Purpose or the goals it wants to achieve in the key profit areas, you might find it difficult to get excited about the work you are doing. If, however, you have developed a sense of purpose as a result of your relationships with leaders, coworkers, and customers, you can help by demonstrating this purpose in both action and language.

Perhaps you work in a real estate firm where some seek to maximize their commissions, even at their clients' expense. You and some of your colleagues find greater meaning and satisfaction in helping people buy and sell properties that are best suited to their needs rather than those that result in the biggest paycheck. By setting your own standard for others to observe and pursuing your purpose unabashedly, you provide an example that others, including leaders, may emulate. In this way you can begin to establish a purpose in an organization that has lost or never defined one or that has inadvertently begun following an unhealthy purpose.

PASSION PLAN WORKSHEET #3

Step Three: Clarify Purpose   How

A. The Organization's "Big Purpose":	Define what you see as the organization's primary purpose or mission. Like passion, the Big Purpose should stem from the heart of the organization as well. Some questions to consider when defining the Big Purpose include: • What is the most important accomplishment for the organization to achieve? • What differences does the organization want to make in this world? • What does the organization want to be most remembered for accomplishing? • Why does the organization exist?

Passion Plan Worksheet #3 (cont.)

B. **Ways the Organization's Core Passions Can Help Achieve Its Big Purpose**

 1.

 2.

 3.

Identify ways that the pursuit of the organization's passions can help to achieve its Big Purpose. Look for possibilities rather than limitations of how its passions can work together to serve its Big Purpose (consider all aspects of the Passion Profile). Some questions to consider when deciding how passion factors in to achieving the Big Purpose include:

- How will we ensure that the organization's passion will work to its ultimate benefit?
- Do any of the organization's core passions factor in to achieving its Big Purpose?
- What are some unique ways the organization's passions might be carried out?

Passion Plan Worksheet #3 (cont.)

C. **Profit the Organization Would Like to Experience from Its Passion Pursuits:**

Category   Specific Examples

List the major categories and specific examples of how the organization would like to Profit from its passion pursuits. Some categories to consider include:

- Financial
- Interpersonal
- Internal (Employees)
- External (Customers and Partners)
- Professional
- Spiritual
- Civic
- Humanitarian

Passionism...

"You may think that passion defies planning, but it needs structure to thrive and endure in your organization."

CHAPTER 6

Step Four: Define Actions

Planning for Passion-Inspired Change and Growth

We must ask where we are and whither we are tending.
—ABRAHAM LINCOLN

By now most leaders and associates are antsy for action. They have identified their organization's core passions, clarified its purposes, and are eager to move forward. There is one final step, however, that they must take in preparing to implement passion-based change: they must prepare a plan of action, a step-by-step strategy for aligning the organization around passion.

Many organizations engage in strategic planning, but few integrate passion into the process, much less make it the focus of their efforts. The action plan you will devise here will be different. It will focus on passion as the catalyst for change and the source of future excellence. It will target ways to capitalize on existing passions and to nurture new ones. Most important, it will delineate possible paths to lead the organization from where it is to where it could be. It will connect visions of the future with conditions of the present and provide a blueprint for putting passion to work.

Why a Plan?

I rarely encounter leaders who question the value of planning. Plans articulate goals and help organizations achieve them—at least in theory. But many organizations define and follow plans that lead them in the wrong direction. Usually this happens because they fail to factor passion into the mix. It is as if the organization is setting out on a road trip, map in hand, but with an empty fuel tank. It may have a vision of its destination but no means of reaching it.

This is not to say that raw passion cannot propel the organization forward in the absence of careful planning. Consider the case of PSS/World Medical. Founded in 1983 by a trio of former medical supply salesmen and managers, the company grew from zero revenues to $2 billion in fifteen years. Much of the company's later growth can be attributed to passion-based planning, but its early success occurred largely in the absence of a plan.

As CEO Patrick Kelly notes in his book *Faster Company,* the owners' early expectations were simple: "First, we wanted the company to survive. Then, we wanted to get our incomes back to where they had been before we started the business. Once the company was successful, we wanted to make money. We figured that's what it was all about: making money" (Kelly and Case, 1998, p. 58). Although they established money as their goal, they were motivated by two core passions that define the company to this day: giving customers what they want and having fun. When in 1988 they had reached their financial goals, they realized it was time for something more.

PSS stands for Physician Sales and Service. The business is not glamorous. As Kelly notes, "We're in a business that's about as ordinary as they come." The company distributes medical supplies to doctors' offices and nursing homes, and X-ray supplies to hospitals and radiology centers. Though its operations seem simple, the company was founded on a revolutionary model. Kelly and his partners knew that most doctors were hostages of the traditional delivery system. They were forced to place large orders that were delivered at two-week intervals, leaving them with cartons full of supplies at times when the distributor felt like sending them, not when they really needed them. PSS would be different. It would offer next-day delivery on orders of any size and offer top-notch customer service. Rather than sending products via a delivery service, PSS would operate its own fleet of vans and establish close relationships between drivers and the physicians' offices they served. The hope was that doctors would be willing to pay PSS's higher prices for the added convenience and improved service.

The model was wildly successful at a time when most believed that there was no room for small, independent companies in the health care field. Defying such skepticism, PSS grew to a $20 million company by 1988. It was at this time that Kelly realized the company had been growing without a plan. Somehow through hard work, luck, and smart operations PSS had beaten the odds, but the company had no idea where it was going. After attending a management seminar, Kelly knew he had to come up with a goal, something that would drive the business into the next decade.

As I mentioned before, PSS's core passions were already in place, but the organization did not have a plan for pursuing them. Kelly set an ambitious goal that most thought impossible to achieve: becoming the first national physician-supply company. Until that time local and regional suppliers had dominated the industry, and the notion that one company could cover the entire country seemed illogical. Not to mention that PSS had only seven offices in one state. Expanding to forty-nine more seemed unrealistic.

Undaunted, Kelly embarked on his mission. He recognized that the key to PSS's growth would be twofold: acquiring other successful suppliers and driving their competitors out of business. So he developed a plan to do just that. The plan entailed raising the necessary capital to make the acquisitions, articulating the goal to the employees, and aggressively moving into new markets. To the shock of many, PSS reached the goal by 1995.

But the plan extended beyond this. Before reaching this milestone, the PSS leaders established another goal. They would reach $1 billion in sales by 2001. Again, this seemed overly ambitious, as the company's current revenues were only $170 million. But true to form, PSS reached its goal three years ahead of schedule.

Part of achieving that goal was expanding the company's base of operations. PSS/World Medical, the new name of the organization, is a holding company that includes four divisions: Physician Sales and Service, Diagnostic Imaging, World

Med, and Gulf South Medical (a nursing home supplier). As the name implies, the new goal is to become the first world-wide distributor of medical products, and you can be sure that there is a plan in place for getting there.

The PSS experience teaches leaders a valuable lesson. Even a highly passionate organization needs a plan to help it harness its passions and fulfill its purposes. PSS was undoubtedly successful before it came to this realization, but whereas its early success was left to chance, its later success was carefully orchestrated. Planning enabled the organization to move from industry success to industry phenomenon. Kelly notes the critical juncture at which planning entered the picture, "Maybe we could have stayed right there, with $10 million or $20 million in sales and 100 or 200 employees. Many fine companies do. But I think we all had something else in mind" (Kelly and Case, 1998, p. 50).

Scope, Intensity, and Pace

If you have something else in mind for your organization—something more, something better—then you need to create an action plan for achieving it. There are three basic characteristics of the plan that leaders need to consider when creating it: scope, intensity, and pace. Each will be determined by the nature of the change that leaders seek and the level of passion that is already present in the organization.

Scope

For some organizations, acknowledging passion and planning to use it will be just the edge they need to jump into overdrive, to begin performing at an exceptional level. In such cases, the changes required may be minor. Certain areas of the business may already be excelling while others need only slight modification. For other organizations, wholesale changes may be necessary to produce results. Every area of the business may require transformation. Leaders need to be aware at the outset of the scope of changes they are attempting. In doing so, they should consider the following areas:

Structure. Does the current structure of the organization support its core passions? If not, how can it be changed to accommodate them? Does management need to be reorganized? Do divisions need to be redefined?

Operations. Will the basic nature of the business change? Will it change its product or service offerings? Will it move into a different field or approach the same one in a different way? How will its operations be affected by these changes? What will be required to implement them?

Finances. What will the changes require financially? Do they require the organization to abandon current revenue streams in order to develop new ones? If so, how much are leaders and shareholders prepared to invest in the process? How much change can current resources support and for how long?

Leadership. Are leaders prepared to make the necessary changes? Do they understand the core passions? Will they need to be trained? Are key leaders willing to dismiss those who do not support passion-based initiatives?

Employees. What will be required of employees? Will their roles or duties change? How much effort will it take to educate them on the passions and purpose of the organization? What kind of programs can the organization implement to help them make the transition? What will leaders do if employees do not respond favorably?

Customers. Will customers be affected either immediately or in the long run? Do the changes require their support? How will the core passions be communicated to them, if at all?

Partners. Will following core passions require the organization to change its alliances or partnerships? Will it change the way business is conducted with other organizations? Will new criteria be established for forming future relationships?

In all probability, passion-based change will affect each of these areas. To what extent and to what effect will be determined by the scope the action plan entails. Leaders may be wary of making changes in too many areas and limit their plan accordingly. Or they may be ready to make broad revisions and prepare a more expansive plan. Whatever the case, the changes targeted must be significant: they must open the doors to passion.

Intensity

If leaders are in tune with their organization—with its operations and its associates—they should have an inherent sense of what kind and degree of change it can handle. In defining the action plan, they need to be mindful of intensity. Even though when passion is present, the organization will be capable of more, there is a point at which too much change can be overwhelming. In this case the group will just grind to a halt rather than blazing forward. To assess the intensity at which they can introduce changes leaders should consider the following factors:

The emotional state of associates, including leaders. How prepared are they for change? How drastic will the required changes be for them? If fear or caution prevail, then people must be won over before changes are pursued too aggressively. Failure to do so can result in alienation and discontent. If associates are already enthusiastic and prepared to perform, then leaders may feel confident attacking change with heightened intensity.

The impact on operations. Can current operations sustain significant change without crumbling under the pressure? Do changes need to be approached with restraint to allow systems to catch up with passion or can they be implemented with gusto to capitalize on mood and opportunity?

Financial viability. Does the organization's current financial condition permit it to confidently tackle changes, or will it need to strengthen its reserves as it works toward passion-driven improvement?

Regardless of where the organization stands now, as passion grows intensity will naturally increase. Leaders should be optimistic and enthusiastic at the outset, but also frank. They should approach the action plan at an intensity that feels sustainable but challenging.

Pace

This is similar to intensity but indicates a commitment of time rather than energy. How quickly is the organization prepared to implement changes? Can it make immediate and pronounced changes or will it need to approach them gradually? The pace of the action plan will be determined by the same factors that define intensity. It can, of course, change over time. As passion becomes more familiar, associates may be prepared to move forward more quickly and alternatives for funding and operations might arise. If changes are pursued too rapidly, leaders can also choose to slow them down.

The correlation between scope, intensity, and pace is usually direct. In other words, when organizations are prepared to make sweeping changes their scope is broader, intensity higher, and pace faster. When they are cautious about it, their scope is narrower, intensity lower, and pace slower. This is not always the case, and ultimately only the leaders of the organization can determine its need and readiness for change.

To help leaders begin, they should place the organization in one of the following categories:

- *Aggressive*—ready to aggressively pursue core passions by making rapid and sweeping changes
- *Moderate*—ready to devote considerable energy to pursuing core passions by making successive and significant changes in many areas
- *Reserved*—prepared to pursue core passions by making gradual yet progressive changes in at least one area

Passion Review

The organization must create an action plan that reflects its readiness for change. The plan should entail a scope, intensity, and pace that challenge the organization, yet are achievable.

Scope is the breadth of the plan.

Intensity is the time and energy it requires.

Pace is the rate of change it requires.

The category leaders select is a guideline for creating the organization's action plan. The changes they target should thus be consistent with it. If the organization is reserved, planning for broad change in the immediate future would be foolish. By the same token, if it is aggressive, slating few and narrow changes might rob associates of enthusiasm or commitment.

Developing an Action Plan

Using scope, intensity, and pace as a guide, leaders are prepared to develop the organization's action plan. The plan has three basic components: the long-term plan, the contingency plan, and the short-term plan. All three components are guided by a set of overall considerations, so I'll address those first.

Key Strategic Initiatives

When it comes to preparing an action plan, I advise leaders to view it as a comprehensive vision of change rather than a laundry list of things to be done. To help them do this, I encourage them to group the actions they propose into categories that I call "key strategic initiatives." An initiative encompasses multiple actions directed at a common theme, such as an individual core passion or a function within the organization. If leaders have identified delighting customers as a core passion, then all activities related to customer service would be included in a single key strategic initiative. This would include employee training programs, changes in distribution practices, and the formation of new business alliances. Similarly, if leaders have recognized technology as a core passion, then all actions dedicated to fueling this passion should fall into one key strategic initiative.

Each key strategic initiative can include actions in many areas of the business. Because these actions serve the same end, they should be linked and viewed as integral to each other. In preparing the plan, leaders may want to account for multiple approaches to each initiative that can be tested simultaneously. As the plan is implemented, approaches that are effective can be continued, while those that are not can be modified or abandoned.

Long-Term Planning

Organizations can only take steps today if they know what they are seeking to achieve tomorrow. For this reason, leaders should create a long-term plan before addressing more immediate issues. This plan should establish goals that are consistent with the organization's purposes and are to be achieved at different intervals, such as three, five, and ten years. As PSS/World Medical illustrates, the best goals are those that challenge the organization and to many seem unattainable. While not completely unrealistic, they force the organization to stretch itself, its capabilities, and its spirit to meet them. By allotting specific time frames, the plan provides opportunity for the growth and improvement necessary to achieve them.

As part of its passion for social responsibility, Ben & Jerry's has established a goal of being environmentally responsible in its operations. Though this sounds like it might be easy, especially given the company's previous success and its commitment to its passion, leaders realize that it must be a long-term goal. The business could never have been built if it did not rely on production processes that create waste, ingredients produced and supplied by others, and packaging materials that are potentially hazardous to the environment. The changes required to achieve maximum environmental responsibility cannot be made in one day. If it attempted to do so, the company would be forced to stop producing ice cream (some alternatives simply do not exist yet) or suffer financial ruin.

To ensure that neither happens, Ben & Jerry's has taken a long-term approach to its environmental actions. A number of years ago it set a goal of using unbleached containers for packaging its products. The organization saw this as a major contribution to its environmental agenda because the bleaching process releases large amounts of carcinogenic dioxins into the environment. Because there was no readily available unbleached paperboard packaging for ice cream, Ben & Jerry's was forced to take a slow but aggressive approach. At great but sustainable expense, the company convinced the necessary manufacturers to supply the unbleached materials; in 1998, it became the first frozen food company to offer its products in unbleached containers.

The introduction of the Eco-Pint (as the new container is called) represented a major milestone in Ben & Jerry's long-range plan, but there are many more slated for the future. The company has set goals for reducing levels of solid and dairy waste and supporting sustainable agriculture through its relationships with dairy farms. Each of these long-term goals, which can be considered part of the company's environmental initiative, determines the short-term actions that leaders take to begin to bring them about.

Brazosport Independent School District (BISD) also recognizes the value of long-term planning. At one time the organization's long-range goal was to be "exemplary" in its performance by raising the level of student performance across racial and socioeconomic divisions. Now that is a reality. Today its objective is to be "exemplary and beyond." Brazosport seeks to be not just the best school district in Texas but the best school district in the United States.

Superintendent Gerald Anderson realizes the key to achieving this goal is consistent, sustainable efforts made over a period of years. The district sets one-, three-, and five-year objectives as milestones for working toward its long-term vision. These objectives give associates and customers (students, parents, and the community) something they can hold onto, something concrete they can envision. This is critical because people can be intimidated by ambitious goals. Achieving a single, monstrous goal seems more likely when viewed as a series of smaller, less formidable accomplishments. Consider BISD's vision in the early 1990s. It seemed unattainable to many. But it became possible as year after year, each school made incremental improvements and the district as a whole drew nearer to its goal.

In setting the organization's long-term plan, leaders may not be sure exactly how they will accomplish it. This is a challenge they can tackle on a monthly, weekly, or daily basis, one that will become easier as passion is developed in the organization. What matters more is that they articulate specific and achievable goals for years to come. Mind you, when I say achievable, I do not mean easy. The goals need only be possible, not probable. As the organization begins working passion into its operations, opportunities will arise and options will become evident, making the unlikely a reality.

Contingency Planning

Because things do not always go as planned, and because some things are beyond the control of the organization, leaders need to include contingencies in both their long- and short-term plans. What this means is that for every major action, leaders anticipate possible outcomes and plan their responses for each.

When EarthLink founder Sky Dayton started his ISP, he might never have predicted that it would grow to serve over a million subscribers in five years. On the other hand, he and his management team took every action to ensure that it would. In the volatile world of high-tech, long-term planning seems an oxymoron. EarthLink's leadership can plan for the future, but the specifics of how they get there will be determined largely by the rapidly changing landscape of their industry. The organization tries to drive changes in technology and consumer tastes, but even so it cannot predict where both will lead it. To remain competitive, leaders must plan across a wide variety of scenarios.

One variable early EarthLink executives might have factored into their plan was outside ownership. Often small companies sell a piece of the pie to larger organizations that can help to fuel their growth. EarthLink did this with Sprint Communications in 1998, when the telecommunications giant acquired 28 percent of the company. As a result of the deal, EarthLink added Sprint's 130,000 Internet subscribers to its customer base. Subsequent to the Sprint deal and facing serious competition from much larger organizations, EarthLink anticipated the need to merge with or acquire other ISPs. Thus its long-term plan accounted for the possibility of a deal like the MindSpring one. It also accounted for the possibility that such a deal could fall apart and targeted alternative courses of action if it did.

As the newly merged organization enters the new millennium, it has established a bold goal of becoming the number one Internet service provider in the world. Given that AmericaOnline's membership is more than five times EarthLink's, this is a tall order. Certainly it has contingencies built into its action plan to prepare it for the journey ahead. These might include acquiring or being acquired by another organization, making the move from traditional dial-up Internet access to high-speed alternatives such as DSL, responding to new technologies, both anticipated and unanticipated, forming alliances with software and hardware companies, and reacting to the relative success or failure of multimillion-dollar marketing campaigns.

Though high-tech firms face more rapid change than those in other fields, all organizations confront choices and must respond to evolving conditions. Leaders cannot be expected to foresee all potential events and outcomes in the organization's future, but they can prepare themselves to respond with confidence. Besides outlining specific courses of action, the contingency plan provides an exercise in constructive response. It helps leaders envision possibilities and evaluate probabilities so that when new developments arise they will be ready and understand how to act in accordance with core passions.

Short-Term Planning

The last element of the action plan, the short-term plan, is certainly not the least. While long-term goals are critical, they will never be achieved if changes are not made to engage passion at some level in the next day, week, or month. Even if the organization is categorized as reserved, it can begin to make passion-based changes immediately. A simple shift in leadership's outlook can have a profound effect, as can changes in office atmosphere or communication style.

Aggressive approaches are always riskier in the short term, but their potential benefit is also greater. In making short-term plans, leaders must be careful not to throw the baby out with the bathwater, so to speak. They cannot compromise current strengths in the face of unproved passions. Given a basic level of prudence, however, they should not be afraid to stretch the limits of the organization in fighting for its growth.

Looking back to the experience of Wainwright Industries, we can see the value in planning for immediate and significant change. After seeing the light at the Ritz Carlton, the company's leaders returned with an agenda. First, CEO Don Wainwright addressed employees and told them things were going to change. Simple as that. He did not go into elaborate detail—he didn't have it to give. He delivered the message that mattered: from that point forward managers were going to trust employees, and employees would play a vital role in improving the organization. This was a clear, no-nonsense communication of the core passion that would drive the most pronounced change: sincere trust and belief in people.

The other immediate move the Wainwright leadership made was to implement a training program aimed at winning trust while also extending it. Through the program employees would be given the opportunity to improve their basic math and vocabulary skills as well as interpersonal skills such as listening and sharing. By investing in employees with time and money and emotion, the leaders demonstrated that the passion-driven change they were introducing was more than just a song and dance. It was real. It was there.

Wainwright's actions demonstrate the three considerations that are essential to short-term planning. In creating their plans, leaders should seek to do the following:

Drive out passion-draining factors. With his speech, Don Wainwright lodged a direct attack on the force that posed the greatest threat to his organization's core passion: fear. If employees could trust they would not be censured or criticized for making suggestions, then they would be empowered to offer them. In the same way, organizations can take the immediate steps necessary to drive passion-draining forces out of the workplace. This might entail abandoning offensive policies, opening channels of communication, or terminating relationships with unsupportive partners—anything that makes it easier for passion to enter the organization.

Introduce passion-inspiring factors. Just as leaders must plan to move the detrimental out, they must target ways to move the beneficial in. For Wainwright this was accomplished by the introduction of training programs. Employees were given immediate opportunities to improve themselves and at the same time develop trust in the organization. This in turn gave them a platform for building on the core passion in their own ways. They acquired skills they needed to formulate and share their ideas, which then became the foundation for the company's continuous improvement program. Leaders should consider any step that will demonstrate and inspire passion. Possibilities include employee workshops and changes to the physical environment.

Make action a reality, not a fantasy. Many organizations spend a lot of time pondering changes they could make to become better, but few actually make them. To ensure that these visions of change become a reality, the first steps that leaders include in their plan need to be ones they are prepared to take. If the short-term plan is too ambitious or complicated, change may never begin. Even the most well-intentioned group can lose its courage if it aims too high too fast. This is not to say that ambition has no place in the short-term plan. The Wainwright team was certainly ambitious—but it was also prepared to take the leap and begin to change. No matter how minor the change or how the small the step, if it begins the process of passion-based improvement, it is monumental in importance.

Planning for Success

Creating the action plan certainly is a challenge in itself. The success the organization seeks to build by following it is an even greater one. To ensure that the plan in each of its aspects—long term, contingency, and short term—will be effective, those creating it need to be sure it is proactive, flexible, and opportunistic.

Passion Review

Elements of the Action Plan
- *Key Strategic Initiatives*—multiple actions directed at a common theme.
- *Long-Term Plan*—a plan that establishes goals to be achieved at different intervals, such as three, five, and ten years.
- *Contingency Plan*—a plan that anticipates possible outcomes of actions and responses for each.
- *Short-Term Plan*—a plan that establishes immediate changes to engage passion in the organization.

Be Proactive

I have advised pragmatism in preparing the action plan, especially the short-term element, because a lack of it can result in immediate failure. It is critical, however, that leaders do not view this as an excuse to plan below the organization's capacity for change. They must be proactive in their design and challenge its current limitations.

We have seen how this has worked in a number of cases. McLeodUSA started with nothing less than the goal of creating "spectacular opportunities" for its employees and began working to do so from its inception. Brazosport Independent School District made no bones about the significance or viability of its goals. Rather than looking for excuses, it charged forward mindful of, yet undaunted by, all the apparent stumbling blocks. PSS/World Medical set big, bold goals and planned big, bold steps for reaching them.

While a certain degree of caution is necessary, timidity does not pay when it comes to passion. Leaders must always remember this and be earnest in their planning.

Be Opportunistic

Many people are familiar with the rags-to-riches story of Gateway Computer. Started in a small South Dakota town, it grew from a farmhouse operation to a multibillion-dollar business within a decade. Founder Ted Waitt created the business to provide people with personal computers built to meet their individual needs. Rather than mass-producing one computer and forcing it on desperate consumers, Waitt envisioned a company that would give consumers what they really wanted and needed. Moreover, he wanted to humanize a field that was often cold, impersonal, and overly technical. He hoped his organization could serve as a trusted guide to its customers; that it could help them understand and benefit from the often-confusing world of technology.

Fulfilling this role of trusted guide has led Gateway to expand beyond built-to-order personal computers and beyond the borders of South Dakota. The company is now what one vice president terms a "full service technology solution integrator." While it still builds PCs and ships them out in the familiar black-and-white spotted boxes, it also provides software, service, support, training, Internet access, and portal capabilities for its customers. The organization aspires to build richer, more lasting relationships with them by providing this wider offering of services.

One of the keys to Gateway's success has been its ability to appreciate opportunity and plan around it. It might have stuck with its original model, but then it might not have become the number one seller of personal computers in the United States. Instead it viewed changes in technology and customer needs as possibilities not only for growth but also for carrying out the core passion of being the trusted guide. Leaders realized that humanizing the digital revolution did not stop with the box, it began there.

The company also sought opportunities to grow and improve. By moving its administrative headquarters from North Sioux City to San Diego in 1998, leaders opened themselves to widespread criticism. Many felt that the shift to a more cosmopolitan locale was a betrayal of the small-town Midwestern values the company embraced. On the contrary, Waitt and his team saw nothing but opportunity in making the move. They realized that exponential growth required increased leadership and that finding that leadership would be difficult in their original location. As the 1998 annual report relates, "Staying in the Midwest was the right move in 1985. Thirteen years later, branching West toward the largest technology and marketing talent pool in the U.S. was the right move."

Gateway has consistently seized opportunities, some of which it has planned, others which it has not. It demonstrates what I like to call *positive opportunism*. Rather than fearing changes in the industry, it welcomes them. Rather than waiting for developments to occur, it instigates them. All organizations are capable of this type of behavior. By integrating a sense of opportunism into the action plan, leaders can establish a self-fulfilling precedent. They will start the process of creating opportunities from within and prepare the organization to embrace those that come from without.

Be Flexible

Opportunism requires flexibility. In today's survival-of-the-fittest environment, businesses must not only adapt in the face of change but also thrive on it. Clarke American was founded over 125 years ago and became a leader in its industry as a result of a passion for quality and customer service. It has remained a leader because of its flexibility in pursuing these passions.

At a time when many feel printed checks are a thing of the past, Clarke American knows otherwise. After focusing on one area for so many years, it understands its business and its customers better than anyone. This is why the organization has committed itself to producing a superior product—its checks—and providing superior service to the customers who order them, which includes banks and individual account holders. Leaders do realize, however, that changes are occurring within their industry and that in order to grow the organization needs to address these changes.

In the mid-1990s, Clarke American's leadership commissioned a strategic study to determine where the financial industry was going. They used the results of this study to determine their plan for the future. The basis was simple: Clarke American would stand by its core competency—the check—and focus on developing value-added services around it. Their research told them this was what their customers wanted and they knew it was what they could best offer them.

By retaining this focus and building on its core passions, Clarke American has watched scores of competitors fall by the wayside. More impressively, it has achieved double-digit annual growth at a time when its remaining competitors have slipped to an average 3 percent increase in revenues. You might be surprised, though, at the ways the organization has stood behind the check. They are neither staid nor static.

When competitors were focused on moving into other areas such as electronic commerce, Clarke American redoubled its focus on printing. It partnered with Xerox to develop a new laser printing technology that gives it greater capacity and flexibility in printing. To discover the ways it could expand beyond printing but remain focused on check-related services, the organization listened to its customers. What it heard was that bank employees were undertrained and dissatisfied and that account holders were confused. As it passed this information along to its institutional clients, leaders learned that the banks were desperate for help.

Overwhelmed by the chaos of constant mergers, acquisitions, consolidations, and downsizings, many banks were, and still are, finding it difficult to meet their customers' needs in a satisfying manner. Clarke American began training them in the finer points of customer service and also serving as call centers for them. With the necessary training, Clarke American's telephone representatives are able to deliver the same level of service on behalf of the bank that they do on behalf of their employer, and in so doing, everyone wins.

This type of evolution might have been neither obvious nor welcome to a lesser organization. But Clarke American's leaders demonstrated a wisdom and flexibility that enabled their success. For them this flexibility did not mean jumping blindly from business to business, it meant seeking alternatives that capitalized on their core competencies. They did not dismiss the new printing technology as an unnecessary or expensive step that could be skipped in the transition to electronic banking. They embraced it because they understood their market. They did not dismiss fielding phone calls as detracting from their basic business. They welcomed it as a valuable addition to it. Now others who did not share their opinion are clamoring to build similar services in their organizations.

Clarke American's example summarizes what all organizations need to remember in developing their action plans: keep passion at the center. Being flexible, opportunistic, and proactive are only relevant if they build on core passions. Clarke American has adapted when others could not by remaining true to its passions and planning ways to build upon them. Gateway Computer has achieved its success by remaining ever committed to its passion of being a trusted guide. Its actions have sustained it and provided a means of pursuing it in the future.

Leaders can use the worksheet at the end of this chapter to create an action plan for their organization. Associates can similarly use it to create a personal action plan for introducing change in their individual positions or departments.

Actions for Associates

You can create an action plan for your department, your team, or just yourself, depending on your sphere of influence. Your plan can incorporate all the elements of the organizational plan, namely the long-term, contingency, and short-term plans. The scenarios you envision and contingencies you plan for will of course depend on your position. There is a chance that the changes you plan will not be accepted or tolerated by leadership, in which case you might be forced to alter or even abandon your plan. There is a distinct possibility, however, that they will produce positive results and therefore be welcomed. You will not know for sure until you put them into action in Step Five.

PASSION PLAN WORKSHEET #4

Step Four: Define Actions   **How**

A. The "Scope" of the Organization's Actions:	Decide which aspects of the organization to target for action. Typically, the scope of your actions should address each area in which you hope to Profit. Some questions to consider when defining your scope include: • Does the current organization structure support its core passions? • How will operations be impacted? • Is the organization prepared to invest in passion pursuits? • Are leaders ready to make the necessary changes?
B. The "Intensity" of the Organization's Actions	Determine how intensely the organization is willing and able to pursue its passion. Some questions to consider when deciding the "intensity" include: • Are associates and leaders prepared for a change?

Passion Plan Worksheet #4 (cont.)

	• Can current operations sustain performance and transition concurrently? • How much of the organization's energy is it able to devote to pursuing its passion? • Is the intensity at a comfortable level, rather than overly enthusiastic or overly optimistic?
C. The "Pace" of the Organization's Actions:	Define the pace at which the organization can pursue its passion. Some questions to consider when deciding the appropriate pace include: • How aggressively do leaders want to pursue core passions? • How pronounced are the potential organizational changes? • Does the organization have the patience and stamina to move forward at a slower pace? • How much risk is the organization willing to take? • How much urgency do the senior leaders feel?

Passion Plan Worksheet #4 (cont.)

D. **Action Steps to Move the Organization Toward Its Passion (Both Short and Long Term)**

Action Step (Task/Activity)	Start/End Dates	Purpose and Potential Benefits for This Action

Organize your actions into sequential, manageable tasks and activities. Points to consider:

- Key strategic initiatives
- Planned schedule (target dates) for starting and completing actions
- Why do this task or activity and how does the organization hope to benefit?

Consider the following questions when defining your actions:

- Who else will be affected by the actions the organization plans to take?
- Why is this action important in pursuing the organization's passion?
- What resources will be needed to complete the action?
- What does the organization have to consider "not doing" in order to complete an action?

Passion Plan Worksheet #4 (cont.)

			• How will the organization know that it has been successful in carrying out each particular action?

E. Contingency Plans Include:

Action Step (Task/Activity)	Start/End Dates	Purpose and Potential Benefits for This Action

Focus on developing contingency plans for the most critical actions. Make the necessary people aware of these plans. Consider the following:

• What specific threats and opportunities influence the actions the organization plans to take?
• How will the organization deal with unanticipated obstacles or opportunities?
• What can be done to prevent these potential obstacles from occurring or to allow these opportunities to occur?

Passionism...

"When your work is a reflection of the desires of your heart, you will perform with exhilaration and without regret."

CHAPTER 7

Step Five: Perform with Passion

Translating Passion into Performance in the Workplace and Marketplace

There are risks and costs to a program of action. But they are far less than the long-range risks of comfortable inaction.
—JOHN F. KENNEDY

As he looks forward to the new millennium, Wainwright Industries CEO Don Wainwright marvels at how far his organization has come in the past decade, "We look back now and think how did we ever get by with those products?" Though the metal products his company produced ten years ago were recognized for their superior quality, they do not compare to the current offerings. Much of the improvement occurred as a result of changes in technology and standards throughout the industry, but the factor that has distinguished Wainwright from its competitors cannot be found in engineering specifications or manufacturing guidelines. As Wainwright recognizes, "passion is everything." It has elevated Wainwright Industries from a good organization to a great one.

Passion can be translated into performance. It can transform organizations and individuals from ordinary to exceptional. This is, after all, why you have come this far. By the time you begin the steps in this chapter, the organization should have an action plan in place and its leadership should be prepared to execute it. If you are an associate planning on an individual or departmental level, you likewise should be ready to implement the changes you have outlined. As changes are made, whether at a global or local level, those affected will quickly realize that excitement and excellence go hand in hand and that the organization is capable of achieving more than even the most optimistic supporters imagined. Passion will bring the organization to a higher level: its performance will be heightened both in quantity and quality and its associates will be energized by their involvement.

Blazing a Passion Trail

The organization now stands poised to begin blazing its passion trail. It is critical as the first steps are taken that leaders closely monitor changes and ensure that they are truly passion enabling. To this end, they must be prepared not only to follow the action plan they created but also to amend it as necessary. The plan is the framework for putting passion into action, but it is not rigid or static. On the contrary, it is flexible and dynamic. The milestones set in the long-term plan and the specific actions targeted in the short-term plan give it structure; the experiences that result from carrying it out give it context and meaning. Leaders and associates should therefore be looking for options as they go, devoting themselves to finding those that best fit the organization and its circumstances. To achieve this, there are three things they should do: investigate, communicate, and assess. Each will help define options and determine which is best suited to the organization and its plan.

Investigate

The epiphany the Wainwright leaders experienced occurred as a result of investigation. They knew things could be better, but they were not sure how. They attended a seminar given by a leader who had worked effective changes in his organization. Though their businesses differed, as did the steps they would subsequently take, the inspiration was the same. The premise of sincere trust and belief in people transformed both organizations.

Countless organizations are seeking answers. Leaders attend workshops and seminars, hire outside consultants, and try program after program in an effort to improve. Certainly there is merit in examining what has worked for others; I am a firm believer in the saying, "Don't reinvent the wheel." But most of these efforts fail because they are not grounded in passion. Once leaders have defined core passions, however, this type of investigation can prove fruitful, even invaluable.

You are probably familiar with the term *benchmarking*. It describes a process whereby an organization compares its operations to the practices and performance of other successful organizations and seeks to improve itself by emulating them. Benchmarking can provide a helpful standard for progress if the results it promotes are a reflection of the organization's core passions. Scores of organizations visit Wainwright's Missouri facilities every year to discover what has distinguished it so clearly from its competitors. If these organizations are driven by similar passions—for excellence, for customer satisfaction, for employee empowerment, or for safety—then benchmarking Wainwright makes sense. If, however, their focus is innovation, design, or maximum profitability, then they might be wise to seek guidance elsewhere.

Fortunately for the rest of us, passion-driven organizations are almost always eager to share their secrets with others. This is an inherent characteristic of passion: it is not selfish. It bursts forth from those who possess it, and is contagious to those who don't. Disney Institute was founded to help individuals explore their passions and to show others how Disney has benefited from its passions. Again, the keys to its success might not apply to every organization; but to those driven by a passion for customer service, learning how Disney has translated its passion for the "guest experience" into superior performance in its markets could prove more effective than months of experimentation or technical inquiry.

There are also independent organizations that have established guidelines for improvement and offer valuable advice in making changes. The National Institute of Standards and Technology, a branch of the U.S. government, administers the Malcolm Baldrige National Quality Award, the nation's highest honor for performance excellence. The Institute encourages organizations around the country to apply for the award not only as a means of receiving recognition but also as a step in the improvement process. As part of the application process, organizations receive "300 to 1,000 hours of review and a detailed feedback report on the company's strengths and opportunities for improvement from business and quality experts on the award's mostly private-sector Board of Examiners" ("Malcolm Baldrige National Quality Award").

I have served as a judge for the award and am well aware of the tremendous benefit a Baldrige review offers an organization. Though passion is not an official criterion for receiving the award, I have yet to encounter a winner that does not possess it. Most applicants are driven by a passion for improvement, hence their commitment to a highly demanding and time-consuming process. But underlying this commitment are core passions that relate specifically to the applicants' businesses, including themes such as technology, customer service, employee improvement and satisfaction, and competition.

The point of these examples is that there are resources available to organizations as they begin implementing their action plans. If part of the short-term plan is to introduce a new training program for employees, then learning how others have succeeded in doing the same makes sense. Your organization can learn from the triumphs of others as well as from their mistakes, and by doing so eliminate much of the guesswork that accompanies change. Just remember that exploring options is never a bad idea, only pursuing the wrong ones.

Communicate

As leaders discover specific possibilities for improvement, they must communicate them to those who know and understand the passions and objectives of the organization. This can include other leaders, associates of the organization, trusted advisers, or anyone who can offer an informed opinion as to how they might play out.

While it is the leaders' responsibility to determine the direction of the organization, they cannot do so in a vacuum. Assuming the core passions they have defined reflect the underlying spirit of its associates, those associates can play a critical part in determining how plans can best be carried out. If leaders have set a milestone of increasing production by 50 percent in one year, they would be foolish not to consult those who handle production in finding ways to do it. As long as employees acknowledge the importance of the core passions in their initiatives, then their ideas are worthy of serious consideration.

Customers can offer particularly valuable insight, as their reactions can determine whether the business succeeds or fails. Both GTE Directories and Clarke American consulted customers in determining how they could best shape and pursue their core passions. GTE Directories learned that it had been steamrolling its customers and solicited feedback from them in gauging how to change its practices. Clarke American, which never lost its focus on delighting customers, has grown its business tremendously through its ability to listen. It is acutely sensitive to the wants of both sets of customers—banks and account holders. By aggressively soliciting their opinions, the organization not only discovered ways to improve its business but also created an entirely new service that is fueling its growth into its second century of existence.

Assess

Once they have investigated and communicated, leaders are prepared to evaluate what they have learned and decide how the organization can best approach reaching its milestones. Though others can offer perspectives and insights, only those inside the organization can determine which steps will work best. This does not mean that leaders should choose the easiest road; on the contrary, the best path might be one that requires associates to push themselves harder or in new ways. The decision should be based on an understanding of the organization's strengths and weaknesses and how they might impact its future success.

An organization that thrives on its passion for people would probably not emulate the practices of one that focuses primarily on technology. Neither would a company that wishes to build on its passion for competitive recognition base its actions on those of an organization dedicated to financial profits. This is not to say that people and technology or awards and income cannot go hand in hand, only that what matters to the organization must be the basis of its actions.

Passion Review

As the organization starts performing with passion, it should do the following:

Investigate—find out what has worked for others.

Communicate—share ideas among those who know and understand the passions and objectives of the organization.

Assess—evaluate options and choose those best suited to the organization and its current situation.

Deploying Passion in the Organization

The first step in the action plan can be grand or minute, blatant or subtle. Whatever its size, it should have the same relative effect. It should ignite a series of subsequent actions that bring passion to the fore throughout the organization. I cannot emphasize this point strongly enough: for passion to be effective, it must be shared by associates and supported by the environment. This effect may be achieved slowly or instantly, but the organization will not enjoy the full benefits of passion until it is.

Imagine approaching a Southwest Airlines terminal only to be greeted by a grumpy gate agent, or entering the corporate offices in Dallas to face cold gray walls and emotionless employees crammed into colorless cubicles. You probably can't, because it just doesn't happen. Not that Southwest employees don't have bad days: I'm sure they do. Or that there isn't a wall unadorned with photographs of associates, their families, and even their pets: there might be one in a remote corner somewhere. But the passion that pervades the organization ensures that employees are excited about their work, that they care about their customers, and that their workplaces exude color and vitality. If passion was not prevalent, then any of these factors could be a variable. Customers could not rely on the airline for the service they crave, and employees could not pride themselves in the jobs they do. In short, Southwest would be just another airline!

The Passionate Leader

Passion must start with leadership. Surely it can emanate from other sources, but in creating a passion-driven business, it has to come from the top. Leaders must live and breathe the passions they profess. Could Ben & Jerry's employees develop or share a passion for social responsibility if Ben Cohen and Jerry Greenfield drove around their Vermont neighborhood in gas-guzzling luxury vehicles, joined discriminatory country clubs, or owned vacation properties in countries ruled by repressive governments? Could Southwest employees get excited about freedom if they were not allowed to make decisions without the permission of supervisors? Could MindSpring employees believe in the core value of frugality if founder Charles Brewer flew in a private jet and received a hefty salary? The answer to all these questions is an obvious no. If leaders do not exude the organization's core passions, associates will have no reason to believe they are real or worth working for.

Passion does not trickle down but rather surges forth from leaders. As Brazosport Independent School District superintendent Gerald Anderson told me,

> I believe with all my heart in what we do. It is contagious with people. They want that kind of leadership. They want somebody that can make them motivated to do their job. And that's where passion for what you do is absolutely critical, not only to the success of the organization, but also to the continuous improvement of the organization. If leadership is going to focus all associates of the organization on the vision and get them motivated and committed, then they must be motivated. They must be committed. They must be able to speak with passion as proof of what the organization can do.

Leaders cannot be tentative or hesitant. The moves they make in deploying the action plan do not need to be earth-shattering, but they must be authentic. They must be made with conviction. Although techniques and practices may change as the plan unfolds, the passion that fuels them must remain constantly evident in leaders' actions.

Aligning Associates

While passion in leaders is essential, it is meaningless if not shared by associates. Without their support, the goals established in the action plan are mere wishes. Associates' energy and commitment are the foundation of the organization's performance and the key to its progress. To ensure results, leaders must immediately and directly seek to align associates with the core passions they have identified.

Though winning associates' support can be a challenge, the battle is mostly won when leaders exemplify passion. Unless the core passions are completely foreign to the organization, they will resonate with most associates. They may build on inklings people have already felt or reflect feelings that drew them to the organization in the first place. Seeing these passions promoted and embodied by leaders will in most cases unleash the passion within employees, or at least plant the seeds for its growth.

The most important and effective practice leaders can adopt in aligning the organization around passion is to establish clear and constant communication. Associates cannot be expected to share a passion they are not aware of or that they do not understand. To this end, leaders should address associates frequently both in person and via correspondence such as memos, e-mail, and company newsletters. Herb Kelleher, CEO of Southwest Airlines, visits numerous Southwest sites each year to deliver his "Message to the Field," which includes a summary of the past year's accomplishments and challenges for future years. After delivering his address, he opens up the floor to employees and answers all their questions individually.

Patrick Kelly, CEO of PSS/World Medical, has an even more ambitious traveling schedule. He visits each of the company's 107 branches twice a year! During his meetings with employees he offers a $2 bill to anyone who will ask a question in an effort to get associates talking about the company, its passions, and its goals. Referring to PSS's core passions, he says, "I've got to get up in front of them as the number one cheerleader and spread the message of customers and fun, customers and fun. It's that simple."

Mobile CEOs are not the only way to establish effective communication in the organization. Southwest publishes on a regular basis an employee newsletter, aptly titled *LUVLines,* that reinforces its core passions for associates. Its in-flight magazine, *Spirit,* also sends the message home for both customers and employees.

Beyond these basic forms of communication, leaders can create programs for the express purpose of educating associates in the core passions of the organization. Of the organizations profiled in this book, no less than half have established internal "universities" or training programs to promote and strengthen passion in their employees. Though as you will learn in the next chapter, these programs have multiple purposes, the most compelling is the articulation of the organization's motivation and direction to associates at all levels.

As measures are taken to increase employees' awareness of core passions, there will be those who simply cannot share them. If associates understand that these passions are the foundation for the business and that they will not be compromised, those not on board will usually choose to leave. I call this practice "self-ejection"—and will describe it in greater detail in the next chapter.

Although the departure of these associates helps to keep passion on track, the introduction of new associates based on their support for the core passions is an even more effective means of aligning the organization around its core passions. The leaders of McLeodUSA realize that the greatest enabler but also the greatest obstacle to their success is people. The opportunities for growth in terms of technology and opportunity are limitless, but McLeodUSA cannot achieve them if it cannot find people to fuel its progress. And the people it finds cannot be just any people; they must be people who support the company's core values—growth, integrity, relationships, and passion—and can truly appreciate the "spectacular opportunities" it wishes to offer them. Recruiting and interviewing efforts immediately establish the company's core passions, and candidates are screened on their perceived ability to uphold them and dedication to doing so.

McLeodUSA is certainly not alone in its practices. Most of the organizations discussed in the pages of this book do the same. Recognizing the critical importance of shared passion in employees, Southwest Airlines CEO Herb Kelleher has been quoted as saying, "We can teach the job—we can't teach the attitude."

Some find passion-centered hiring more challenging than others. Ben & Jerry's does not, for example, hire on the basis of commitment to social progress, though it has considered working such a criterion into its hiring process. What the company does find, however, is that because it is so vocal about its passions outside the bounds of the organization, it attracts people who already share them.

This is true at all levels, from factory workers to CEOs. When Ben & Jerry's was searching for a new leader, a man who at first glance might have seemed an unlikely candidate approached them. As the founders explain in their book,

> Perry [Odak] sought out the company because of his excitement about combining social endeavors with a growing, profitable business. Perry's previous position was at a gun company, and the media made a flap about the apparent conflict with Ben & Jerry's stand in favor of reducing gun violence. What the media neglected to mention was that Perry had been a consultant at that company for nine months out of a twenty-five-year career, and they made hunting rifles, not handguns. We spent a great deal of time talking with Perry about our company's values, and we were as excited about his alignment with the company's mission as we were about his business acumen [Cohen and Greenfield, 1997, p. 188].

Since his hire in 1997, Odak has proven a passionate champion of the organization's social mission. Through his management expertise, he has grown the business while also increasing its commitment to social mission.

When Gateway began its search for senior management in the late 1990s, existing leaders knew that those it selected had to share the company's core values and its passion for not only humanizing the digital revolution but also for creating a very human organization. Current CEO Jeff Weitzen and Executive Vice President Dave Rabino were so excited about the opportunity that stood before them that they made a pact.

While flying cross-country to assume their new positions, they agreed that the organization they were going to lead would not succumb to any of the traditional bullying practices of big business. Unlike many billion-dollar businesses, it would be decent, humane, and fair. They sealed their pact with a handshake.

Weitzen and Rabino were not creating a new culture at Gateway, they were strengthening an existing one. Because the company had so clearly expressed its core passions, both knew what they were getting into, and—more important—were thrilled by the opportunity. They were aligned from the start.

Building a Passion-Inspiring Environment

A critical part of deploying passion in the organization is creating the conditions in which passion can thrive. Not surprisingly, this includes the physical environment. If employees are physically uncomfortable or forced to work in spaces that drain their energy rather than increase it, they will find it difficult to experience passion on a day-to-day basis.

One of my favorite sayings with regard to this principle is "Your butt's connected to your brain." I came across it in an article about GSD&M, the Austin, Texas, ad agency that handles clients such as Wal-Mart and Southwest Airlines (Imperato, 1997, p. 140). GSD&M is renowned for its creativity and leaders acknowledge that employees are only inspired to create when their environment supports "thinking outside the box." The article sums up this theory with this phrase: "Where you sit determines what you think." I would extend this to include "Where you sit determines what you think *and* what you feel." To stimulate passion and foster creativity, GSD&M created Idea City, a self-contained community of workspaces modeled on the world's most inspiring and energetic locales.

Businesses that hinge on creativity are not the only ones that can capitalize on passion by creating stimulating work environments. Manufacturing plants are spaces that must meet strict safety requirements and are traditionally not viewed as hotbeds of innovation. Wainwright Industries has discovered that there is emotional value in these seeming limitations. Safety is the number one priority at Wainwright and employees play an active role in making continuous improvements to the system. The facility reflects the organization's passion for safety and serves as a constant reminder to employees of their shared commitment to safety. All employees, including the CEO, wear the same white uniforms. Floors and machines are spotless. Workspaces are clearly delineated and well lit, as opposed to the cavelike atmosphere that characterizes many factories. Don Wainwright explains that together the employees and facilities "exude perfection."

Another area of the Wainwright building reminds employees of another core passion: customer satisfaction. "Mission Control" is a room devoted to monitoring the company's success in meeting customer needs. Two walls bear plaques, each displaying the name of a customer and the "customer champions" assigned to it. Above each plaque is a flag: green if the company is meeting its goals in pleasing that customer, red if it is falling short. Another wall bears five plaques and flags, each relating to one of the organization's measurement indicators: safety, internal customer satisfaction, external customer satisfaction, product quality, and business performance. These visual cues serve employees as constant reminders of the passions that define the organization and provide an actual incentive to improve performance.

There are an infinite variety of ways leaders can shape physical spaces to inspire passion. Southwest acknowledges its passion for its people throughout its corporate headquarters. As I mentioned earlier, most walls are covered with framed photographs of associates, their families, and even their pets. Lest there be any doubt of the role employees play in sustaining Southwest's core passions, a glass wall surrounding the elevator shaft is engraved with this message: "The people of Southwest Airlines are the creators of what we have become—and of what we will be. Our people transformed an idea into a legend. That legend will continue to grow only so long as it is nourished—by our people's indomitable spirit, boundless energy, immense goodwill, and burning desire to excel. Our thanks—and our love—to the people of Southwest Airlines for creating a marvelous family and a wondrous airline." How could any employee fail to be uplifted by reading this?

Obviously the steps leaders can take to create an engaging environment depend on the nature of the business and the core passions of the organization. Brightly colored walls might not be appropriate in a factory, and high-powered lighting might not promote the right feelings in a health spa. There are some general guidelines leaders can follow, however, in ensuring that associates are energized by their environment:

- *Make it engaging.* Surround associates with visual reminders of core passions.

- *Make it comfortable.* Ensure lighting, coloring, and furnishings facilitate concentration and creativity rather than stifling them.
- *Make it appropriate.* Be sure workspaces are well suited to the types of work performed there.
- *Make it inspiring.* Create conditions that help associates view their work as unique and important rather than dull or monotonous.

Often leaders are confused by these suggestions. Though they seem obvious to many, they are a stretch of the imagination to others. In an era of anonymous cubicles and fluorescent lighting, creating excitement in the workplace is an anomaly. Many fight to overcome the limitations of stuffy or drab facilities but with little effect. I cannot impress upon leaders strongly enough the necessity for associates not only to be comfortable in their environments but also to be stimulated by them. Any discomfort is a distraction; any dull or uninviting space is an opportunity wasted.

For some organizations, building a passion-inspiring environment might necessitate changing facilities or radically redesigning existing ones. For others less dramatic changes might be in order. Whatever the current state of the organization's facilities, leaders must key in on maximizing the potential for passion to flow freely. For Gateway this even meant moving the corporate headquarters halfway across the country. Though those in North Sioux City are passionate about their location and the values it had come to symbolize, leaders realized that in order to attract key management they needed to settle in a more dynamic job market. This is not to say that many of the new Gateway leaders could not be happy in South

Dakota, or that they do not share the Midwestern values Gateway is built on, only that they are more likely to perform in a technology-driven environment. On the newly named Tech Coast they are reminded by why humanizing the digital revolution is so important and afforded greater opportunities to witness the impact of their passion on their customers and their industry.

Creating Passion-Driven Policies and Practices

The policies and practices of the organization can also prove a valuable tool in aligning associates with core passions. In keeping with Southwest's passions for having fun and "coloring outside the lines," employees are encouraged to wear shorts and sneakers to work. This "extreme" casual dress policy serves a distinct purpose. As Colleen Barrett, executive vice president of customers, explains, "A tie cuts off the circulation from the head to the heart, and since Southwest is a company run with the heart . . . we don't allow them."

Barrett's comment highlights the need for consistency between the passions and the reality of the organization. If policies contradict core passions, then associates are likely to be confused and skeptical. As part of its newfound passion for "sincere trust and belief in people," Wainwright Industries got rid of its time clocks. After all, how could employees feel they were trusted in performing their jobs if they could not be trusted in reporting their work times? Though Southwest has guidelines for employees to follow, they are given the freedom to make decisions on the spot that are in the best interest of the customer. They can do so with the confidence that the company supports them, because it acts in accordance with its passion for freedom.

PSS/World Medical gives its employees similar freedom in making decisions. All employees, from executives to sales-people to truck drivers, carry business cards bearing their name and the title "CEO." Official CEO Patrick Kelly explains why this is so important in upholding PSS's core passion for serving the customer, "When you're standing in front of the customer, you *are* the CEO. You have the power to do whatever it takes to satisfy the customer." PSS also proudly refuses to publish a policy manual, shunning the bureaucracy and closed thinking such manuals promote.

While this kind of freedom might not work in all organizations, it is a powerful example of passion in action. Leaders need to remember that sometimes it is the littlest things that have the biggest impact. Simple things such as dress codes, attendance policies, and break-room rules can convey messages that actively defy core passions. Bigger issues such as the definition of job responsibilities and protocol for dealing with customers can also squelch commitment and enthusiasm in employees if they do not reflect the passions professed by leadership. On the other hand, practices and policies that communicate and reinforce core passions enable associates not only to share them but also to strengthen them within the organization.

Promoting a Passionate Outlook

All these things—communication, education, environment, and policies and practices—contribute to the building of a passionate outlook within the organization. When passion permeates all aspects of operations, associates, like leaders, begin to talk the talk *and* walk the walk. They become excited about core passions—and perform in accordance with them. They develop faith in leadership and enthusiasm for goals. They stop finding excuses and start looking for solutions.

The associates of Brazosport Independent School District offer a powerful example of this. As I described in Chapter Four, the district eliminated race, ethnicity, and socioeconomic status as a factor in student performance. After a few years of intense and dedicated effort, teachers and administrators succeeded in teaching basic skills to students of all groups, not just those traditionally favored by the educational process.

The irony in this is that many other districts around the country face fewer challenges but accept defeat as an inherent part of the system. Schools in my own area send home letters citing the importance of parental involvement in public education. They blame poor performance on parents' lack of involvement in their children's homework, on their failure to contribute funds for extra programs, and on their lack of participation in classroom activities. The attitude is "we could, if only you would. . . ."

BISD's attitude is "we can." Fueled by their passion for empowering all students, associates do not view parents as the key to student success. The job of educating students is theirs and theirs alone. As one elementary school principal told me, "Yes, parent involvement is very nice. But my parents are people in poverty that work shift work if they work at all. Their concern is not going and cutting out bulletin board letters for some teacher. I quit judging the parents long ago, because Ward and June Cleaver don't go to school in the new millennium. Beaver had a great situation, but there are no Beavers in my classroom." She accepts circumstances rather than being intimidated by them. She tackles the challenges they present with enthusiasm and confidence because the passion of the organization is alive and thriving within her.

Passion Review

Deploying passion in the organization should entail the following:

- Demonstrating passion in speech and action
- Aligning associates with core passions
- Building a passion-inspiring environment
- Creating passion-driven policies and practices
- Promoting a passionate outlook

The associates of any organization can be filled with this same spirit. When core passions are demonstrated and cultivated consistently and openly, associates begin to assume them as their own. Their outlook is one of conviction and empowerment, and there is little that can sway them from achieving the goals of the organization.

Peak Performance

Aligning the organization around passion creates the conditions necessary for peak performance. This term is often used to refer to individuals but is also relevant to groups. To better understand it—and its ramifications in the workplace—let's examine it from both angles.

In Individuals

Noted psychologist William James wrote, "The human individual . . . lives usually far within his limits; he possesses powers of various sorts which he habitually fails to use. He energizes below his *maximum,* and behaves below his *optimum*" (James, [1902] 1977). Though most of us can attest to this on a personal level, we also know that there are times when we transcend our normal limitations and perform on an elevated level. Abraham Maslow (1968) defined these moments as "peak experiences," and more recently Mihalyi Csikszentmihalyi (1991, 1997) has characterized them as "flow." Regardless of the terminology, the implication is the same: heightened performance.

When performing at our peak, we lose our sense of time. We are usually surprised afterward that so many minutes have passed. We perform effortlessly, as though on autopilot. Something seems to take over and we are more efficient, more capable than our abilities would normally suggest. We also feel at once more alive and more powerful. Our senses are heightened and we tingle with an energy we cannot explain. We feel invincible, in complete control of the task at hand.

Imagine the possibilities for the organization if it could inspire its associates to perform at their peak on a consistent basis! This may seem an unlikely possibility, since for most of us incidents of peak performance are few and far between. But this does not need to be the case. There are a number of factors critical to triggering peak performance. The first is that you are engaged in something that is important to you. This is where passion comes into play. Obviously the things that matter to us are the things that inspire emotion within us. If employees share the passions of the organization, if they truly matter to them, then the groundwork is laid for peak performance.

The second factor is that you are trying to accomplish a specific goal or reward. For associates of an organization this might involve completing a project in a specified time, receiving recognition from leaders for their efforts, or receiving a positive customer review. Whatever the challenge, there must be some standard by which they can gauge their ultimate performance.

The third factor is focus. Peak performance is predicated on concentration. Energies and faculties must be centered on the activity at hand. If people are distracted or troubled, they will be prevented from performing well. This is why the physical and emotional environments are so critical to success.

The implications for the organization are clear. By engaging associates in activities they are interested in, providing them with specific goals and incentives, and creating conditions in which they are inspired and free to concentrate, leaders can elicit their peak performance on a regular basis. I am not suggesting that every employee can be in flow every minute on the job, but they can have consistent, sustained peak experiences if they are actively and meaningfully involved in living the core passions of the organization.

In Groups

If individuals can be induced to perform at their peak, then it follows that groups should be able to do the same. The challenges in facilitating collective peak performance are greater, however. Different associates have different concerns and preferences. What is distracting to one associate might be motivating to another. One might view the task at hand with indifference while another is naturally excited about it. To overcome these potential problems, leaders must create maximum alignment with core passions.

For associates working in the same functional group, there should be common ground in interest, ability, and motivation. Given the right conditions, these people can work together to reach their shared goals and simultaneously perform at their peak. If there are pockets of resistance or certain individuals prevent others from finding flow, then the associates who are not aligned must be helped. They may require further education or training to understand core passions or perhaps need to be moved to an area where their individual passions will flourish.

Core passions are also the forces that unite associates across functions. Ben & Jerry's learned this recently when it faced a seemingly impossible situation. The company had ninety days to create, produce, and market a new product line in order to be prepared for the upcoming selling season. This meant coming up with names, concepts, and package designs, testing ingredients, and getting the new flavors off the production line in record time. The director in charge of this formidable task knew that his team alone could not handle the demands placed upon them, so he sought help throughout the organization. An associate from operations offered an idea that became the foundation for the new line. Why not build on the success of existing flavors by mixing or swirling them together to create new flavors? As the director told me, "Everybody loved this idea and took a part of it. Every department stepped in and said 'We can make this happen.'" The result was the delivery of the highly creative "Two Twisted" line ahead of the deadline. The new flavors include Half-Baked, a combination of Chocolate Chip Cookie Dough and Chocolate Fudge Brownie; Monkey Wrench, a blend of Banana and Peanut Butter Cup; and From Russia with Buzz, a swirling of White Russian and Coffee Coffee Buzz Buzz Buzz.

While the specific skills and tasks of the Ben & Jerry's associates who created this line differ, their motives do not. I have consulted for many organizations that profess a passion for creating great products or providing superior customer service, but cannot rise above interdepartmental squabbling to produce the ends they seek. Such a problem indicates to me two things: strife is preventing associates from performing at their peak, and the core passions are getting lost somewhere in the process.

Organizations that are strongly aligned with core passions experience peak performance on a global level. While not every aspect of these businesses is perfect at every moment, most function more smoothly, produce a higher quality and quantity of work, and meet their goals more readily than those that are not centered on passion. Their effectiveness builds over time because peak performance is self-perpetuating. Associates are uplifted by their successes and enthusiastic about creating more. The channels to creativity, innovation, and consistency are opened and the organization achieves group flow.

Performing in Parallel

As organizations become aligned with core passions, they become more powerful. They become capable of achieving multiple goals—not in sequence but simultaneously. I call this *performing in parallel.*

Traditionally we have been taught that to excel in any one area we must give it our undivided attention. I disagree. With passion at work and peak performance factors in place, organizations can achieve pronounced results in many areas. Consider Ben & Jerry's. Its focus on social responsibility has in no way impeded its creation of great ice creams. On the contrary, the company's commitment has fueled its creativity. In 1997 Ben & Jerry's introduced Phish Food, a flavor inspired by an alliance with the rock band Phish. A nationally recognized group from Vermont, Phish is also committed to raising awareness of social issues. Band associates were eager to work with Ben & Jerry's toward this end. The company created the flavor—chocolate ice cream with marshmallow nougat, caramel swirl, and fudge fish—and the band agreed to contribute the royalties it receives from sales to a nature foundation. Phish Food is currently Ben & Jerry's number three selling flavor, behind perennial favorites Cherry Garcia and Chocolate Chip Cookie Dough. In this way it has not only served the company's social mission but contributed to its bottom line as well.

Southwest Airlines's passion for freedom has resulted in widespread accomplishment. It has won the devotion of thousands of adoring customers, created legions of loyal and satisfied employees, and made the organization the only consistently profitable airline in the world. This passion has bred pride and enthusiasm in employees and raised the level of their performance in all areas. For example, the airline does not profess a passion for safety, but safety is an integral part of preserving freedom. It has established one of the most impressive safety records in the industry because its maintenance personnel are passionate about serving the organization and its customers. It is almost as if safety, a critical factor in any airline's success, is a byproduct of passion rather than an objective.

When the organization embarks on its action plan, leaders and associates alike will notice this phenomenon. They will learn that by harnessing passion they can pursue many goals without compromising any. Southwest does not forgo safety or profits by focusing on fun. Ben & Jerry's does not sacrifice creativity or quality by concentrating on social issues. Drawing on core passions, their possibilities for success expand and the effort required to achieve them diminishes. Positive results, often unexpected, begin popping up across functions and throughout all levels of the organization.

Making Passion-Based Decisions

Sometimes an organization implements an action plan and immediately encounters difficulty in following it. Early struggles can occur because leaders and associates are not yet making decisions consistent with core passions. As changes are made, members of the organization must commit to honoring the spirit of the plan. They do not need to follow it blindly: we have already discussed the need for flexibility once things are under way. They do, however, need to remain true to the passions that define it. Abandoning passion, even temporarily, for the sake of pragmatism, pressure, or quick profits will deter the organization's progress and prevent it from capitalizing on its most valuable resource.

This can be confusing for many organizations because often the choice that is most consistent with core passions is not the one that makes the most sense. In these cases leaders must remember that it is the heart and not the head that must prevail. Gateway faced such a decision in 1997 when it was evaluating ways to expand on its built-to-order business model. At the time industry experts were looking to the Internet as the key to the future. They maintained that Web-based sales models were the way to go, and augured the death of brick-and-mortar computer sales. Never one to flinch in the face of conventional wisdom, Gateway flatly rejected this advice and launched an aggressive campaign to build a line of retail stores called Gateway Country.

One vice president recalls the reaction this action received. "We had every financial and industry analyst in the world shaking their heads. And the media absolutely killed us. But we stuck with the idea because we knew what our customers wanted." In listening to their customers, Gateway executives knew that most people were still not comfortable buying direct. Many wanted to see and touch what they were buying before forking over their hard-earned money. So the company built stores—lots of them—investing millions of dollars in an effort most analysts thought foolhardy and backward.

What critics did not appreciate was the fact that the concept behind the stores was revolutionary. Gateway's passion for being the consumer's trusted guide meant that it would not force mass-produced, generic computers on unsuspecting customers. It still stood firmly behind its commitment to meeting the individual's needs. The result was a store that displayed samples but did not stock inventory; a staff of experts that sought to help and guide customers rather than meet sales quotas or push last year's models out the door. With its Country stores, Gateway redefined the retail environment. Customers could kick the tires, get advice, and place an order for precisely what they wanted, when they wanted it.

Gateway's decision to remain true to its passion despite the potential dangers has resulted in phenomenal success. The stores have increased earnings exponentially and poised the organization for even greater growth in the future. Competitors are struggling to replicate the Gateway Country model, but so far have failed to match Gateway's success.

Passion-based decisions are not always aggressive in nature. Southwest Airlines has declined time and time again to change its business in ways critics argue would bolster its growth. Other airlines have emulated Southwest's no-frills, quick-in-and-out model as a means of providing low fares to customers. But most have been tempted to branch out by offering longer flights on bigger planes. The result has been failure. Southwest remains committed to freedom for its customers. Adding transoceanic flights would require buying jumbo jets, stocking meals, and losing efficiency in turn-around times, all of which would result in increased fares. Though the company might be able to sustain its business and even build a new one, it would do so at the expense of those it set out to serve. It would deny them the freedom that has become the emblem of the airline and at the same time kill the passion that originally gave it life.

As passion becomes the motivating force in the organization's operations, making this type of decision becomes easier. Gateway's leaders had been bucking convention for more than a decade when they opened their first Country store. Southwest officials had to remain fiercely committed to their passions to get their first plane off the ground. Both organizations have learned that risk is an inherent part of business, and only those who accept it will succeed. They also understand that a passion-informed risk is a calculated one. It is grounded in the very forces that give the organization strength and vitality and is safe inasmuch as it upholds them. Passion-driven businesses realize they face a greater risk in denying core passions. They know that doing so jeopardizes the lifeline of the organization, squelches its potential, and trades long-term fulfillment for temporary benefits.

After kicking off the action plan, the organization should begin to reap the rewards of its efforts almost immediately. It will not achieve all its goals in one day or week or month, but it will be energized and begin gaining momentum. As long as core passions are communicated and upheld in word and action, there will be a palpable change in the atmosphere, a new spirit of enthusiasm that will drive progress and fuel success. The organization will have taken a bold and definitive step on its self-defined road to Profit.

Actions for Associates

You will encounter all the challenges and benefits I have described in this chapter when embarking on your own action plan. If passion becomes a part of your daily work, your performance will improve and your actions will be noticed. You should be prepared for both praise from those who appreciate your passion and criticism from those who do not. As you move forward with your plan, you will gain a sense of its chances for success. Your need for flexibility is even greater than your leaders' because you are subject to their authority and must heed their wishes if you are to continue in their employ. If they do not accept the changes you feel you should and must make, then you might find it necessary to find an organization with leaders who do. Hopefully, this will not be the case and the example you set will be followed by your coworkers, gradually elevating the overall operation at a grass-roots level.

PASSION PLAN WORKSHEET #5

Step Five: Perform with Passion	How
A. Ways That We Can Investigate Our Action Plans:	Investigate ways that the organization has succeeded (and failed) in pursuing its core passions. Consider the following: • Are all actions equally important? • Have we researched other organizations that have succeeded in pursuing the same passion? What lessons did they learn? • What organizations or associations exist that relate to our organization's passion? What do they have to share that can help us?
B. Ways That We Can Communicate Our Action Plans:	Determine who inside and outside of the organization should be kept informed and solicit their opinions. Although feedback is always valuable, remember that you are ultimately responsible for your actions and choices.

Passion Plan Worksheet #5 (cont.)

	Consider the following: • Have we communicated with trusted confidants about our actions? • Have we identified someone who might act as a trusted coach who can give us honest feedback while we are pursuing our passions? • Are we clear on the messages we want to communicate to those around us who might be affected?
C. Ways That We Can Assess Our Action Plans:	Evaluate what you've learned from investigating and communicating your action plans. Make appropriate refinements, but avoid taking the easy path. Consider the following: • What changes do we need to make to the actions we have planned? • Have we discovered an action we need to take that was overlooked? • Do we need to reprioritize the actions that were planned?

Passion Plan Worksheet #5 (cont.)

D. **The Passion-Inspiring Environment We Need to Create:**	Identify the changes the organization needs to make to create the conditions in which passion can thrive. Consider the following: • Have we surrounded our associates with reminders of our passion? • Are the physical conditions conducive to progress? • Are we spending time with customers and associates that feed our passion? • What organizational routines and habits do we need to refine?
E. **Create Passion-Driven Policies and Practices:**	List the needed organizational policies and practices that can help align associates around core passions and keep them focused on pursuing the organization's action plans. Consider the following: • What policies or practices will help us experience and live our passion?

Passion Plan Worksheet #5 (cont.)

	• Which policies and practices prevent us from experiencing our passion? • Are there policies or practices we need to have that are not defined? • Do our senior leaders display behaviors that support the organization's pursuit of its passion?
F. Ways to Realign Around the Organization's Passion:	List the activities, people, experiences, and behaviors that can help the organization realign itself around its core passions and pursue its action plan. Consider the following: • What activities do associates participate in that promote passion on the job? • How can we get work groups and teams to incorporate organizational passions into their efforts?

Passionism...

"When employees are passionate about their work, the organization thrives."

CHAPTER 8

Step Six: Spread Excitement

Sparking Commitment and Enthusiasm in Employees, Partners, and Customers

Would you persuade, speak of interest, not of reason.
—BENJAMIN FRANKLIN

Once passion is present in the organization, it becomes contagious. All the participants in the business—employees, partners, and customers alike—sense it and respond to it. This is a natural process: enthusiasm begets enthusiasm. The challenge is to find ways to spread passion to achieve maximum and lasting effect. This involves concerted efforts to communicate and develop it both internally and externally. By actively promoting and managing passion in all three groups, the organization will benefit in ways leaders may never have imagined. It will win support, inspire loyalty, and gain invaluable energy as associates from each group share in the excitement passion creates.

Inspiring Employees

Never has there been a time so ripe with opportunity, full of promise, or replete with choices for employees. And never has there been a time when the organizations that employ them need their vitality, creativity, and energy more. Competition is fierce, customers are demanding, and conditions are changing rapidly. For some, the quest is first to keep up and only then to excel.

While different organizations face different circumstances, all share the need for people. Clark McLeod, CEO of McLeodUSA, writes, "Very early on, those of us who created this company came to the realization that 90 percent of what was required for success centered on people. We had a plan. We had money. We had access to the best technology. We had an unlimited marketplace. People, by far, represented the biggest challenge, the greatest barrier we faced. Attracting and retaining people—people who individually and collectively are 'stars'—appeared to be the only factor that could limit our success" (McLeod, 2000, p. 3).

These sentiments are mirrored in the words of PSS/World Medical's Patrick Kelly: "People are a faster company's only real asset. You want—you need—the very best people you can find. You don't really care about experience, because you'll teach them to do things your way. But you do care—a lot!—about the attitudes and values they bring with them. You can teach people *how* to accomplish great things. It's much harder to teach them to *want* to accomplish great things" (Kelly, 1998, p. 122).

Clarke American's Human Resources Champion of Development told me the same thing: "The key to our success, now and in the future, is our people. Our competitors can duplicate our technology, they can duplicate our products and they can duplicate our processes. But they can't clone our people."

I could provide quote after quote attesting to this fact. Winning organizations realize that they don't just need people, they need passionate people. Patrick Kelly and Southwest CEO Herb Kelleher agree that the excitement and enthusiasm that characterize passion are the most valuable qualities in an employee. Their organizations hire people first and foremost based on passion and only second based on skills. The reason is simple: when employees are passionate about their work, the organization thrives.

Nurturing Their Passion

As I discussed in Chapter Seven, there are many steps organizations can take to hire people who will share the passions of the organization and subsequently be passionate in carrying them out. These include clearly communicating core passions in recruiting efforts and including passion-based criteria in the interview process. You may think that once passionate recruits are on board, the work is done; the business is free to take off. To the contrary, the true work has only just begun. The organization must seek to help employees grow in their passion. This includes helping them more fully understand and experience the organization's core passions and finding ways to incorporate their individual passions into their work.

This challenge also holds true for existing employees who have lost their passion or have never shared the core passions of the organization. Though some may simply not belong, others just need guidance and encouragement in discovering and developing passion on a personal level.

The bottom line is that if organizations want associates to be passionate about their work, they must be passionate about helping them. At the Disney Institute leaders go to extreme lengths to make sure employees (who are called cast members) are experiencing the very same emotions they want them to pass on their guests. One way of doing this is providing them with opportunities to experience the Institute from the perspective of a guest. New reservationists are invited to stay in the resort for a night so they can understand what they are selling to their customers. They dine in the restaurant, enjoy the spa and fitness center, and attend programming, and all the while are treated to the same level of warmth and enthusiasm extended to guests. One Institute leader explains the motivation behind this practice, "It would be a false expectation to think people could stay passionate about something but then not let them try it themselves. . . . We just think it's really important that people stay connected to who we are and what we do so they can communicate that passion to our guests."

This type of experience helps employees understand the passions of the organization and engages them on a very personal level. They see that the organization is willing to invest in them and as a result are motivated to invest their energies and abilities toward its progress.

Providing ongoing training and education is another way organizations can effectively invest in their associates. Instructing them in the core passions is important, but this is only part of the process. More lasting in impact is training geared toward personal development. This may seem illogical, as strongly as I argued the need for alignment with core passions in the last chapter, but consider it in these terms. Someone gets up before you and preaches his passion. He gets excited, jumps up and down, and convinces you that he is onto something. You leave the room energized and excited about what he has said. A few weeks later you are still on board, but find your enthusiasm waning slightly. As time passes, you fall out of touch with your initial emotions and forget why you were so excited in the first place.

What if, instead, this man shared his passions, but then invited you to sit down and explore your own? What if he helped you get in touch with the forces that move you and the things that excite you personally? What if he helped you target careers that allowed you to build on these passions or advised you how to develop them? Would you not gain a deeper appreciation for his passions by understanding your own? Would you not be more enthusiastic about helping him since he had helped you?

Training employees can give them not only the skills but also the emotional tools they need to perform at their peak and derive fulfillment from their work. If leaders can get them excited about their personal potential, then they will be excited about the organization's as well. At Southwest's University for People employees can take classes in leadership, customer service, career development, team performance, and personal development. Leadership classes focus on the company's history, its values, and its passions, but also help individuals identify their own strengths and potential areas for growth. Other course offerings teach employees time and life management techniques, public speaking, and interpersonal skills.

PSS also operates its own university. Most of the classes focus on job-related skills, but their underlying purpose is to improve the individual. Like Southwest, PSS conducts personality tests to help people gain a window into themselves. On occasion sales recruits realize that selling is really not for them and decide to pursue different careers. Similarly, some of those who enter the university's Leadership School find that despite the initial appeal, a leadership role is not for them.

Contrary to what you might think, PSS does not give up on these people. It subscribes to what is commonly called "right fit" placement, or placing people in jobs that best match their passions and abilities. This is an invaluable and necessary practice because sharing the passions of the organization does not guarantee employees' success. They must be passionate about the specific job they do in order to excel. What this requires from the organization is a commitment to the individual, not just as an employee but as a person.

We strive to do this at my own firm. A few years ago I had a young man working for me in the desktop publishing department. He was energetic and committed, a valuable addition to our team. But he was not thrilled about his job. Knowing we did not want to lose this employee, his supervisor and I sat down with him and discussed possible alternatives. What we learned was that he had a tremendous passion for competition, which he was actively pursuing in his personal life: he was training for the Olympics! In his professional life, however, he was not able to draw on this passion in his role as a designer. We came up with a plan to help him maximize his passion and improve his performance. First, we agreed to give him more flexibility in his schedule so that he could beef up his training as the Olympics approached. We were thrilled by his goal and proud to support it. Second, he would move to a sales role that would bring out his competitive spirit and provide him with greater opportunity to exercise his passion. The result was what we hoped for. He brought more of his core passion to his new position and went on to compete in the Olympic trials as well.

Though traditionally organizations have sought to match employees to jobs based on their skills, rarely have they done it based on their passions. I think this is a tragedy. There are so many great people out there who have the potential to excel if only given the right opportunity. PSS recognizes this. Southwest Airlines does too. So do most of the organizations I researched in writing this book. If employees are excited about the organization, share its passions, and are eager to contribute, then the organization should be willing to invest in them in two ways: to help people discover their individual passions, and to nurture these passions by placing people in roles that call them out. The results are well worth the time and money required. The organization fills its ranks with passionate, capable associates who make maximum contributions to its success.

An easy way to start this process is to hire from within. Rather than conducting extensive searches outside the organization, many passion-driven organizations start their searches inside. If leaders know employees who are aligned with the core passions and enthusiastic about being a part of the organization, why not give them the opportunity to grow by taking on new roles? It may require time and money up front for training, but will save both in the long run.

Southwest Airlines has extended this policy to include family members of employees. Its nepotism policy is, "We hire 'em." While there are basic requirements any employee must meet, the organization has learned that members of the same family often share the same passions and attitudes, and if one is a good fit, then so are the others. As a testimony to this fact, the company has over eight hundred married couples on its payroll!

Utilizing Their Passion

When associates are excited about the organization and passionate about what they do, the benefits are tremendous. They are happier, more productive, more creative, and eager to come to work each day. Because they are invested emotionally, they are also loyal. Their relationship goes beyond the transactional (work performed for paycheck received). They are committed on a deeper level to the organization and its success.

The passion-driven organization views its employees as associates—as integral parts of the greater whole. It values their contributions and respects their opinions. It knows that their energy fuels its progress and seeks to use it in the most effective ways possible.

For many organizations this translates into giving their associates freedom—freedom to think for themselves and act in accordance with core passions rather than policies. I have already described how Southwest employees are encouraged to use their own judgment in determining how to best serve customers. Not only are they trusted to make on-the-spot decisions, they are also given free rein in expressing their passion. Some flight attendants sing and others tell jokes. Some pop out of overhead compartments and others impersonate celebrities. Not every associate is zany: leaders make it clear they are also free to do things in more traditional ways. But by affording its employees this type of freedom, Southwest achieves something that no other airline can. It delivers what it calls "positively outrageous service" and keeps its customers coming back for more.

Cast members of the Disney Institute are also encouraged to exercise freedom in serving their customers. One of the Institute's goals is creating magical moments for guests, and there is no canned formula for that. To achieve it, the Institute must rely on the creativity and initiative of its associates. The director of the Institute told me about a maid who has worked there since its opening. Now most people wouldn't consider housekeeping a particularly glamorous or creative job. But this particular woman truly loves what she does and is passionate about surprising her guests. Instead of just cleaning a room, she personalizes it. She may arrange stuffed animals kids have left in the room on the bed, or leave a little note welcoming the guests back to the room—small tokens, to be sure, but meaningful nonetheless.

One aspect of giving associates freedom is allowing them to make suggestions for improving the organization. After all, they know the work they do better than anyone. And if they are passionate about it, they will naturally be eager to do it in the best way possible. Wainwright Industries has built its success on the ideas of its employees. In a business where safety and quality are paramount, constant improvement is required. To address this need, the company instituted a Continuous Improvement Program (CIP) to actively solicit suggestions from associates. While many organizations have suggestion boxes, few ever use the suggestions to produce significant change. The Wainwright program is different. Employees are encouraged to implement their ideas first and only then to submit them for organization-wide implementation. Management realizes that ideas have no value if they are not put into action. And action is what defines the CIP. Associates average more than one suggestion per employee per week, which reflects over two hundred changes being made every seven days. That's a lot of improvement!

Clarke American's program is called S.T.A.R., for Suggestions—Teams—Actions—Results. Associates submit process improvement suggestions and are recognized for their contributions. Though not all suggestions are implemented, the program acknowledges the importance of continuous associate involvement in its progress. Southwest Airlines similarly welcomes ideas from associates, though in less systematic ways. CEO Herb Kelleher receives over a hundred letters of suggestion from associates each month. Every letter receives serious consideration and a response from key leaders.

Rewarding Their Passion

An essential part of encouraging passion in associates is rewarding them for expressing it. Leaders can never take enthusiasm for granted and should consistently acknowledge it in meaningful ways. This can involve a wide variety of practices ranging from performance incentives to celebrations.

One practice that is rapidly increasing in popularity is providing employees with ownership. Stock options are an incredibly effective tool for fostering and perpetuating passion in associates. Most employees understand that the potential payoff from stock options far exceeds their gain from salary and benefits. More important, however, stock options give associates a vested interest in the success of the organization. If it benefits from the passion they pour in, then they benefit as well with a growing portfolio.

Traditionally stock options have been reserved for executives, but leaders now realize the need to extend them to everyone. Administrative assistants and assembly line workers are just as critical to the organization's success as executives are, and sometimes their loyalty is even harder to win. Denying them a piece of the pie simply does not make sense.

PSS/World Medical operates by the maxim, "Share the wealth." It rewards all associates with stock options as part of their basic compensation plan. Patrick Kelly boasts that through such ownership, the company has already created a few hundred millionaires. Even truck drivers and salespeople have amassed small fortunes through their service to the organization. Kelly maintains ownership not only ties associates to the business but also creates an extra level of excitement around it.

Beyond its regular plan, PSS gives employees additional ways to earn stock that are directly tied to passion. Once a month each branch of the company takes a field trip of sorts. Associates travel to an offsite location such as a miniature golf course, a go-cart track, or a picnic site, where they eat, play, and participate in a game called the PSS Challenge. During the game associates are called on to demonstrate their knowledge of the company's core passions in amusing and nonthreatening ways. It helps to reinforce their understanding and builds passion around the experience itself. The potential rewards of the game extend well beyond fun, however. Those who attend at least ten of these events in any given year split one million dollars' worth of PSS stock. Most recently, 2,300 employees claimed their share.

Incentives such as this can be effective not simply because they increase associates' net worth but because they validate the passion people bring to the table. Simply throwing employees a bone every now and then may win their commitment temporarily, but it will not encourage them to invest emotionally in the organization. When incentives are built into the system and predicated on passion, they have a pronounced and lasting effect: they engage employees on a higher level and encourage their heightened contribution.

Earlier I mentioned the Wainwright Continuous Improvement Program. The main reward for associates in contributing their ideas is the knowledge that they are making a difference in the organization, that they actually have an impact on its success. The company rewards this contribution materially as well. Each CIP suggestion earns an associate an entry into a weekly drawing for a gift certificate. Those suggestions that address safety, a core passion for the organization, win the associate three entries. This may seem like a small gesture, but it speaks volumes to employees: the company recognizes the importance of their passion and is willing, even eager, to reward it.

Far more compelling, though, is recognition of passion through performance management systems. Wainwright threw out its old rating system when it realized that it was compensating associates based on arbitrary factors that did not reflect its core passions. Now associates are evaluated based on their accomplishment and commitment to furthering these passions. Regardless of their role, they receive raises, but more significantly promotions, by demonstrating enthusiasm and ability in contributing to the organization's atmosphere of trust and its internal and external customer satisfaction initiatives.

By identifying passion as one of its core values, McLeod-USA found a way to officially work passion into its human resources systems. Like Wainwright, it ties increases in associates' compensation to their success in the areas that matter most: growth, relationships, integrity, and passion. The motivation is that if employees are living the core passions of the organization, they are by definition contributing to its progress.

Those who not only demonstrate a commitment to the core passions but also excel in carrying them out receive additional recognition. Every year McLeodUSA sends two hundred employees and their spouses on an all-expenses-paid trip to a tropical resort as a reward for their contributions. Awards are also an integral part of the recognition system. The company holds semiannual retreats at a nearby resort where it presents top performers with plaques, trophies, and—most important—public gratitude.

This sense of gratitude is critical to encouraging passion in associates. They must know that their passion makes a difference. Southwest Airlines is so thankful to its employees it plasters their pictures on the cover of its in-flight magazine, showers them regularly with awards such as Employee of the Quarter, the President's Award, the Founder's Award, the Freedom Fighter Award, and the LUV Award. Since customer service, both internal and external, is a core passion at Southwest, many of the awards recognize contributions in this area. But there are more instances of excellence than the company can acknowledge with certificates. The passion for serving others is so deeply ingrained in the organization that it receives over thirty-five thousand letters from customers commending its associates each year. Rather than merely accepting this praise, Southwest revels in it. Undoubtedly with some help, Herb Kelleher responds to each and every letter. Both the employee and the customer receive his personal thanks. To make sure the accomplishment is not forgotten, the letter is also added to the employee's permanent file.

This kind of expression, from both customer and leader, can be priceless to associates. Mary Tomlinson, director of the Disney Institute, acknowledges that gratitude from guests keeps the passion of its associates thriving. Like Southwest, the Institute receives thousands of letters acknowledging specific cast members. Leaders read these letters in cast gatherings and cascade them through departmental meetings. She says, "In order to stay passionate, if you are a frontline cast member, you just have to believe that what you are doing is making a difference. So we're going to find every way possible to reinforce that belief and make sure you know that the energy you give out every day to our guests is making a difference."

Consistently acknowledging passion and performance in associates creates a celebratory atmosphere at most passion-driven organizations. Every day is an accomplishment as core passions are played out and the organization moves on down its road to Profit. What better reason to celebrate than that? And why not do it on a regular basis? Southwest has to publish a monthly calendar of events just to keep associates apprised of all its celebrations. They include "Spirit Parties," an annual chili cookoff, gong shows, limbo contests, and countless other festivities. Despite what stuffy and shortsighted managers might think, rather than detracting from employees' work, these events generate a level of excitement that enhances it.

Ultimately celebration is about more than recognizing past accomplishments. It is about moving on to new ones. Brazosport Independent School District superintendent Gerald Anderson kicks off every school year with a major celebration that might include a laser light show, fireworks, and live music. At the party he encourages teachers and faculty to take pride in all they have achieved. He then extends a challenge and outlines the goals for the new year. By presenting the challenge in the context of a celebration, he ensures that associates feel empowered. They understand that whatever lies before them, they can do it. After all, they have already done it. They need only draw on the same passion that enabled them to succeed in previous years to succeed in the upcoming one.

Recognizing Passion Gaps

Regardless of the measures the organization takes to spread and maintain passion in its associates, there will be times when some fail to catch on. This can result in what I call a *passion gap.* The gap will usually be evident because the performance of the individual or group will lag behind the rest of the organization.

GTE Directories recently faced such a problem. One of its regional sales divisions was experiencing over 40 percent staff turnover. Morale was low and performance had dropped precipitously. Leaders realized something was terribly wrong and acted quickly to form a Quality Improvement Team (QIT) that traveled to the struggling office to confront the problem. The team organized a "coaching blitz" in which each member was paired with a division associate. One by one the "coaches" listened to the associates and realized what was missing. Somehow over the miles passion had been lost. Associates did not feel part of the organizational family and were not inspired by its commitment to customer satisfaction. The "coaches" immediately set to work training associates, communicating and reinforcing the core passions. Most important, they made them feel needed and appreciated, which allowed their individual passion to emerge. Within months, the division was transformed. The turnover rate improved by 63 percent and associate satisfaction by 171 percent—positively impacting both external customer satisfaction and profitability in the process.

In this case communication was the remedy. There are other times, however, where associates cannot be convinced or inspired to be passionate about the organization or their work. When this happens, there is usually little choice: they must leave. Most often they will depart on their own, finding the environment offensive. This sounds strange, but if you do not share the passion of a group, you're apt to find it, to use the words of one leader, "nauseating." Being surrounded by a bunch of energetic people who get excited about things that are meaningless to you isn't the most desirable of situations. For those who do not self-eject, there is often grounds for termination. If performance evaluations are based on passion-driven factors, then the offending employee will probably fall short and not survive reviews.

Though such cases are extreme, they do happen. If the organization is focused on passion and seeks constantly to build it in employees, disaffected associates will become a rarity. Rather than displaying skepticism and dissatisfaction, associates will exude confidence and enthusiasm. They will be united in their optimism and elevate the organization to new heights.

Passion Review

The organization must continually inspire its employees by doing the following:

- Nurturing their passion
- Utilizing their passion
- Rewarding their passion
- Recognizing passion gaps

Enticing Partners

The benefits of passion are not limited to internal improvement. On the contrary, spreading passion to partners can produce significant positive results. These include the formation of lasting, mutually beneficial relationships, promotion of the core passions outside the walls of the organization, and increased support in reaching objectives.

Ben & Jerry's has experienced all these benefits and more. It has done so not by standing idly by, but rather by actively promoting its core passions in all of its business relationships. In the last few years it has developed a "social mission screen" that all suppliers and distributors must complete in order to work with the company. After reviewing the screen, Ben & Jerry's determines whether the organization is sufficiently committed to similar issues to merit a partnership. The potential partner is not required to be perfect; in fact, a basic premise of the program is to help other organizations improve, just as Ben & Jerry's seeks to do internally. If the organization agrees to work on its shortcomings, then there is room for negotiation.

In one instance, Ben & Jerry's leadership set down an ultimatum with a large and important partner. Women in the organization were grossly underpaid in relation to their male colleagues and were not allowed to rise to senior management positions. If the organization did not work immediately to remedy the situation, Ben & Jerry's would terminate its relationship with the company. Though they were not thrilled in doing so, leaders consented. This type of policy makes Ben & Jerry's what CEO Perry Odak calls a "500-pound gorilla" in the ice cream business. It has risen to a position of power in its industry and is not afraid to wield its power in promoting its passion. As Odak says, "The bigger we get, the more lives we can positively impact."

Though some partners initially find this a hard pill to swallow, ultimately it ends up strengthening relationships. As they begin to reap the benefits of the improvements they are compelled to make, partners begin to share the passion that inspired them. For those who already do, there is additional excitement around the alliance. Not only does the relationship provide income, it lends credibility. Even the smallest of suppliers wear their affiliation like a badge of accomplishment. It demonstrates to customers and other partners that they make the grade. They too can bask in the benefits of Ben & Jerry's passion.

It is no surprise that relationships function more smoothly when those involved share similar motivations. McLeodUSA recognizes this fact and seeks to form partnerships with organizations that sustain its core passions. The company has found that passion-based relationships inspire loyalty and endure far beyond those based on convenience or necessity. As a result the organization is eager to enter into them even if it means spending more. The long-term benefit of a strong alliance is worth far more than short-term financial savings.

Clarke American selects its partners based on their shared passion for customer service. It has no interest in working with financial institutions that are not committed to delighting their customers. For those who show desire but fall short in practice, the organization is eager to share its expertise. By instructing partners in methods that support this passion, it not only wins their devotion, it extends its passion even further into the marketplace.

The newly reenergized Apple Computer chose to make EarthLink its official Internet partner based largely on the ISP's passion. At the 2000 MacWorld Expo, Apple CEO Steve Jobs announced that all of the company's Macintosh computers would offer EarthLink as the exclusive ISP in their Internet Setup Software. Jobs commented, "EarthLink and Apple share a passion for providing the highest-quality Internet access to Macintosh users, and together we're going to do it better than anyone else" ("Apple and Earthlink Form Partnership . . . "). As a result of the alliance, both companies benefit financially when Macintosh users subscribe to the EarthLink service. In effect Jobs has become a passionate spokesperson for Earth-Link. The message he delivers to his legions of loyal followers is twofold. Not only is EarthLink a great company but by choosing EarthLink, you help Apple as well.

This highlights one of the greatest benefits of spreading passion to partners: they help spread it to customers! This holds true for formal partners as well as those connected to the organization in informal ways. Ben & Jerry's executives acknowledge that their products sometimes get more shelf space in supermarkets than other brands because the people stocking the shelves admire the company and share its passions. For the same reasons its products appear frequently on television programs and in movies as props. Executives do not seek this publicity; it stems naturally from the excitement that others share surrounding the organization and its products.

Just as passion creates willing, eager employees, so does it inspire enthusiastic, helpful partners. The organization that understands this can do much to ensure that its partnerships are not only functional but also highly beneficial. Through education, encouragement, and assistance, it can build lasting relationships that enable it to exceed traditional boundaries and achieve a new type of success. Not only will the organization benefit from its involvement, it will also help others move forward along their paths to Profit.

Wowing Customers

If you have ever been excited about a company or its products, you know the power that passion can wield over customers. To excel in the new millennium, organizations must strengthen their internal operations through passion and then aggressively extend that passion into the marketplace. Customers are drawn to passion—in products, in services, in corporate images. They crave it for themselves and reward those businesses that offer it with unparalleled loyalty, necessary profits, and invaluable advertising.

Communicating Passion to Them

Passion inside the organization will naturally be reflected outside it. It will be apparent in the superior goods and services it creates. Organizations cannot assume, however, that letting products speak for themselves is enough. To gain maximum benefit from their passions, they must boldly proclaim them to customers. They must educate customers so they both understand and appreciate the organization and what it is trying to accomplish.

One way of doing this is by pronouncing passions in every statement that issues from the organization. This includes advertising, public relations, sales, and marketing. Each message paints a picture of what the organization is about and presents a valuable opportunity to build excitement around it. Southwest Airlines could simply list its fares or cite convenience in its attempts to win customers, but instead it views its ads as a forum for communicating its passions. In 1973 when Braniff attempted to put Southwest out of business by slashing its Dallas-Houston fares to match those of the upstart, Southwest fired back with an ad in local newspapers proclaiming, "Nobody's going to shoot Southwest Airlines out of the sky for a lousy $13." The ad explained Braniff's tactics and highlighted Southwest's commitment to customers' freedom. Through Southwest's efforts, customers understood that the same price did not mean the same benefits. Southwest appealed to them on an emotional level and won their support. Needless to say, Braniff is the one that's no longer around (Freiberg and Freiberg, 1998, pp. 31–33, 260).

The irreverence of Southwest's advertising also communicates its passion for fun. When a competitor ran an ad claiming that Southwest's customers were embarrassed to fly the no-frills airline, Southwest retaliated in its typical good-natured way. Wearing a paper bag over his head, CEO Kelleher told television viewers he would provide embarrassed customers with similar disguises. Discarding the bag, he extended the offer to the unembarrassed, claiming they could use the bag to hold all the money they saved by flying his airline. This commercial clearly communicated the spirit of fun and freedom that characterize Southwest. After seeing it, potential customers would know that flying Southwest would be something different.

Gateway has used its advertising to articulate its passions in similarly effective ways. A television commercial from the mid-1990s portrayed factory workers assembling the company's trademark spotted boxes. One worker turns to another and asks for a screwdriver. The other worker hands over the screwdriver, and then the entire assembly line comes to a halt. Noticing the sudden quiet, both workers scan the room and then turn to each other. The first says, "thank you," and the second responds, "you're welcome." This spot did not emphasize technology or even service, but Gateway's passion for the human element of its business. It expressed the company's personal, values-based approached to technology and clearly communicated an underlying passion to customers. These employees put a very human face on the "friend in the business" that Gateway slogans proclaimed the company to be.

Gateway has recognized the value in communicating passion to customers since its inception. Choosing a Holstein as its symbol and Holstein spots as the motif for its packaging and brand image was not an obvious move for a manufacturer of computers. But what better imagery to convey the company's emphasis on down-to-earth, real-world relationships than a farm animal? Customers need look no further than the spots to know that the company behind them represents good old Midwestern values and wants to turn something intimidating into something friendly.

Ben & Jerry's, which also for more obvious reasons uses a cow in its marketing, has been one of the most aggressive organizations in spreading its passion to its customers. From the days when their business was no more than a single storefront, Ben Cohen and Jerry Greenfield have been looking for excuses to give ice cream away. In the early years, this was the most direct way they could carry out their passion for giving back to the community. As the organization grew, leaders created new opportunities for social involvement. The company continues to give away free cones in scoop shops on its anniversary, but its efforts extend far beyond that. It contributes free ice cream and the bodies to scoop it at countless charity events around the country. As CEO Perry Odak notes, "We will give ice cream to any charity that is looking for help." Usually efforts are coordinated through retailers that carry Ben & Jerry's products. The benefit in such actions is far-reaching. The charity wins because it makes money. Ben & Jerry's wins because it strengthens its relationships with retailers, generates good will among potential customers, and perhaps most important, gets its products into their stomachs!

Giving back also entails sponsoring events to promote public awareness and further those causes to which the organization is committed. Every summer the company sponsors a free music festival in Vermont—the One World One Heart Festival. Though the ice cream is not free at the festival, customers gain a window into the heart of the organization. They enjoy great music, learn about environmental and social issues, shop for organic T-shirts, and sample some of the most innovative ice creams in the world.

Service organizations have an even greater opportunity for communicating passion than do those focused strictly on goods. Their interactions with customers are not limited to an image projected by a package or an advertisement, but extend to an actual experience between customer and associate. At Disney Institute, guest experiences are defined not by the buildings they stay in or the grounds they walk, but by the interactions they have with cast members. This is why the Institute works so fervently to make each and every interaction "magic not tragic." When guests meet with truly great service again and again throughout the course of their stay, they begin to understand the passion that motivates associates. They realize that the organization is not just about winning their vacation dollars; it is about engaging them and inspiring them. It is committed to them on a personal level.

Drawing on Their Passion

An essential part of Disney Institute's business is spreading its passion for customer service to other organizations. When instructors at the Institute teach classes on guest service, they conclude their program with a session titled "Creating the Magic." During this session, participants learn "the crucial point at which customers develop an emotional attachment to an organization, the point at which an organization moves from creating satisfied customers to loyal customers." What leaders really learn is that customers are not a dead-end street. They do not just fork over their money and walk away. When they understand and share the organization's passion, they get excited. They come back or buy more. They encourage others to do the same. They act as advocates for the organization, and though they are not on the payroll, they begin pouring their energies into it.

This often happens in unexpected ways. Many of the flavors Ben & Jerry's currently offers resulted not from the efforts of employees but from the suggestions of enthusiastic customers. The idea for Cherry Garcia, the company's top-selling flavor, was scrawled on an ice cream lid and mailed in anonymously by a customer who recognized the company's passion for creating unique, fun flavors. The connection to the Grateful Dead, a band that shares many of the organization's social views, reveals that this customer was also appreciative of its passion for social responsibility.

The company receives more suggestions for flavors than it could ever produce. Though it eventually tracked down the originator of the Cherry Garcia idea and made sure that she received her due, the current legal ramifications of using customer ideas are complex, to say the least. For this reason, Ben & Jerry's is currently researching ways to allow its customers to share their ideas more freely and without legal complication. One way involves the company's Web site, which at the time of writing, receives over a hundred thousand unique hits per month. Customers visiting the site do much more than view lists of flavors. They share stories about their experiences with the ice cream, wax poetic about their favorite flavors, and lament the loss of those relegated to the flavor graveyard. They can inform representatives of any "less than euphoric" experiences they have had with the company or its products, play a game called "Make Ben & Jerry Hairy," and print out a replica of the original scoop shop.

All these activities reflect the possibilities that passion-based customer-provider relationships provide. When excitement and good feelings abound between the groups, each stands to draw on the energies of the other and be fulfilled by the association. Consider the example of the Brazosport Independent School District. Associates include the teachers, administration, and school faculties. Customers are the students, their parents, and to a certain extent, the community. BISD associates, who have been unfailing in their passion over the last eight years, have found that their work has become easier thanks to the help of these customers. (Note I say easier, not easy!) Once associates began communicating their passion and getting results, excitement about their enterprise grew. A community that once was critical became adulatory. Businesses that once frowned on the organization's work began throwing celebrations for its associates and proudly proclaiming their success throughout the state. Parents who were once reluctant or aloof clamored to help by donating time and money. Around the district, PTA-funded signboards popped up in front of schools, each proclaiming its namesake as the best of the best. Students developed great pride in their accomplishments and became eager to build upon them. The district became a well-oiled machine that gained momentum as the years went by. The passion and commitment of associates energized customers, and the enthusiasm of customers buoyed associates in their continued efforts. Today, as BISD seeks to be exemplary and beyond, its associates know that they can do so not just by giving to their customers but by drawing from them as well.

EarthLink understands this too. It derives up to one-third of its new customers from referrals by existing ones. The company proudly reminds customers, "It's your Internet" and encourages them to help others claim their Internet freedom—freedom from complicated setups, invasive marketing, and formats that prevent them from easily accessing the content they want. Though EarthLink offers incentives such as waiving service fees for those who make the referrals, their motivation most often is an excitement about the service rather than an exercise in economics. The benefit to the company from this word-of-mouth advertising is tremendous. In a business where success is measured by number of subscribers, each new sign-up is a valuable addition.

EarthLink works vigilantly to keep subscribers once it gains them. Like many service-driven companies, it listens to its customers and strives to improve its service to meet their desires. This is not simply an exercise in tweaking little things here and there, but a concerted effort to view the future of the Internet through the eyes of those using it. Though the organization prides itself in finding and developing tools its customers may never predict, it also understands that their passion for the Internet is just as powerful as the organization's. By discovering what really excites customers and feeds their passion, the company can stay one step ahead of the competition.

By changing its products to reflect customer desires, EarthLink demonstrates the importance of not just listening to customers but of acknowledging them and the passion they seek to contribute. Ben & Jerry's responds to each and every customer letter within ten days of receiving it—no small feat when you consider they receive them by the thousands. This includes responses to wisecrackers who accuse the company of false advertising because there is no monkey in the Chunky

Monkey. To this Ben & Jerry's replies that it believes most people prefer simian-free dairy products, but that it hopes the customer recognizes the association with bananas, which are found in the ice cream. The reply includes a coupon for a free pint, and most likely, Ben & Jerry's has now converted a heckler into a supporter!

For those who offer sincere and heartfelt commentary, the timely response lets them know that the company values them, welcomes their passion, and considers their input vital to its improvement. Herb Kelleher does the same thing by responding to the letters from Southwest customers. Michael Eisner, CEO of Disney, was so impressed by the embroidery that an excited Disney Institute guest sent him that he forwarded it to Institute leaders. They had it framed, and invited the woman out for an official hanging in the Institute restaurant. This was a small gesture, but it reflects the incredible enthusiasm customers have to give when the organization reaches them on an emotional level.

As the organization follows its passion plan, it will find it is not alone in its quest. Employees, partners, and customers can all help it achieve its goals and will be eager to do so if it shares its passion with them. The contributions of each group will move the organization forward more quickly and fluidly than leaders might have imagined possible. Perhaps the most gratifying reward of spreading passion, however, is not the progress the organization makes but the benefit to those it helps along the way. Assisting others—both individuals and organizations—in tapping into their passions not only creates enduring relationships, it strengthens people and builds communities.

Actions for Associates

Even if you are alone in bringing passion to the workplace, others will be affected by your actions. Be sure to share your enthusiasm and energy and to take steps to help those around you discover their own. Although you might not be able to transform your organization overnight, you will have a lasting impact on those who are a part of it.

PASSION PLAN WORKSHEET #6

Step Six: Spread Excitement	How
A. **Ways to Nurture Organizational and Individual Passions:**	Identify ways the organization can orient all its associates to its core passions, as well as help associates incorporate individual passions on the job. Consider the following: • Have we shared the passions that are important to the organization? • Has the organization helped associates identify and experience their passion at work? • What types of passion-related training and educational experiences are provided to associates?
B. **Ways to Inspire and Reward Passion Expression:**	Identify ways that you can inspire and reward others for helping build a passion-driven organizational culture. Consider the following: • How have associates inspired each other to pursue their individual passion?

Passion Plan Worksheet #6 (cont.)

	• What can the organization do to inspire passion-aligned behaviors? • How can one associate's passion inspire someone else to pursue their passion? • What lessons-learned can we use to build up and reward passion expression?
C. **Ways to Spread Our Passion to Partners and Customers:**	Incorporate ongoing actions to continue spreading the organization's passion to partners and customers. When spreading passion, remember the following: • Be enthusiastic • Be genuine • Don't erect barriers • Be consistent • Be supportive of others

Passionism ...

"Keeping passion alive is not just a matter of defending it. It also involves seeking opportunities to expand it."

CHAPTER 9

Step Seven: Stay the Course

Keeping the Organization Centered on Passion

Let me tell you the secret that has led me to my goal. My strength lies solely in my tenacity.
—LOUIS PASTEUR

What a wonderful force passion is! But like most good things, it is not guaranteed. Just because the organization aligns itself around passion does not mean it will stay that way. In a rapidly changing world where businesses are faced with increasing challenges, the passion-driven must seek to sustain the energy that propels them. They must work ardently to preserve their passion and keep associates focused on using it. Only then can they be sure they will continue moving forward toward their Profit as time and circumstance evolve.

The Passion Stimulus

Theoretically, preserving passion should be easy. After all, it feeds itself. When leaders are passionate, associates catch the spirit and spread it among themselves. When they grow excited about their work and the goals of the organization, they become more effective and are energized by their efforts. Collectively the organization becomes more successful and is inspired to achieve even more. A little passion poured in results in a lot of passion coming out, and even more to pour back in.

The difficulty comes when reality intervenes. Leaders and associates can plan for changes and target potential courses of action, but they cannot anticipate the actual impact challenges will have until they arise. Their responses in these situations will determine whether passion survives and the organization thrives or whether both suffer permanently disabling blows.

To prepare for such situations, everyone involved must realize that although passion-driven organizations are motivated and energized, they are still subject to everyday frustrations. They can be bogged down by details, irked by delays, and annoyed by inefficiencies. They can face resistance, suffer setbacks, and encounter obstacles. The critical difference between those who remain centered on passion and those who do not is that they consciously draw on the energy and inspiration passion provides to overcome these obstacles. When things get tough they find renewal in their emotions rather than defeat.

I call this the *passion stimulus*. Organizations that build passion into their day-to-day operations will find that it can sustain them through both good times and bad. It will help them confront problems with confidence and vigor, and prevent them from growing complacent in their successes. Properly nurtured and managed it will be a constant source of revitalization and ensure that nothing compromises the organization on its road to Profit.

Keeping Passion Alive

This may seem like a paradox: passion can keep things going, but somehow the organization must work to keep passion going. Luckily, this is not an uphill battle. Once passion becomes ingrained, it is unlikely to simply disappear. The greatest dangers lie in abusing it, neglecting it, or just plain wasting it. By taking a few basic steps, leaders and associates alike can help to strengthen passion on an ongoing basis and secure it as the foundation of the organization's continued success.

Fighting Complacency

One of the greatest challenges passion-driven organizations can face is what I call the "fat and happy syndrome." They become so successful that they lose touch with the fire and enthusiasm that got them where they are. To put it bluntly, they lose their edge. Though the organizations that fall into this trap may still enjoy and believe in their businesses, they become slow and vulnerable to competitors. To prevent this from happening, organizations must build on their successes rather than rest on them.

Disney Institute is an organization that could easily fall victim to this syndrome. Founded to extend the passions of its parent organization, it started with an advantage most don't have: the Disney reputation. Leaders could have created some interesting classes, sought to match the level of customer service Disney provides, and called their efforts sufficient. And by doing so, they might well have succeeded. But they recognized that their greatest strength was also their greatest potential weakness. Because the Institute bears the Disney name, guests arrive expecting more than they would from a non-Disney facility. As a result pleasing them becomes harder, disappointing them easier. The Institute's leaders thus defined one of their core passions as exceeding guest expectations, or in more practical terms, delighting and surprising their customers. They realized that the key to fulfilling this passion was providing a *higher* level of service and establishing a *deeper* emotional connection than any other similar organization.

Given this focus Disney Institute strives to constantly stretch the limits of its passion. It refuses to succumb to complacency, even though most guests are thrilled with their experiences. By viewing each day as a challenge, regardless of past successes, the Institute ensures that it will retain its competitive advantage and that its passion will not dwindle. One director puts it this way, "We're very much out there, working very, very hard, never for a moment taking for granted that the Disney brand or the compelling programming we're offering alone will be enough. That's why we work so hard at living our passion, because we know it is what will bring guests back again."

Unlike Disney Institute, Brazosport Independent School District (BISD) entered its most recent era as a troubled organization. The legacy it had to build on was one of failure rather than success. In less than a decade Superintendent

Gerald Anderson and his supporters transformed the district and earned their schools the distinction of "effective," a less than glorious term for a significant accomplishment. In educational circles, *effectiveness* indicates parity among racial and socioeconomic groups in student performance. In other words, no student is at a disadvantage academically based strictly on family background. Very few districts in the country can claim this success.

Rather than viewing this accomplishment as a stopping point, the district has made it a springboard for future achievement. It has translated its passion into higher objectives. BISD no longer proclaims its vision as *Exemplary 2000,* but seeks to be *Exemplary and Beyond.* As the district Web site informs readers, its mission "continues to be a journey of people, of passion, and of proof based on the belief that all children can learn regardless of family background, sex, or socioeconomic status" ("21st Century: Exemplary and Beyond"). Having succeeded in teaching basic skills such as reading, writing, and mathematics to its students, the district now seeks to give them the skills they need to succeed in the new millennium, including communication, information literacy, problem solving, and technology skills. It envisions a new type of school where "all students will be held to far higher standards of learning because everyone will have to be prepared to think for a living and everyone will have to be capable of learning many new skills over the course of a lifetime." This is an approach that few of BISD's counterparts can emulate. They have not achieved the initial success necessary to move along these lines.

Passion has enabled BISD to succeed and associates realize its continued importance in moving forward. Superintendent

Anderson says, "I get very, very passionate about why we have to continuously improve and why we cannot rest on our laurels. . . . Because we have attained a level of success where it is easy for people to say we're very, very good. In order to extend our passion, we have to move our training to a higher level to show our people how we can take a very successful organization and make it even more successful." This unwillingness to settle for anything less than the best keeps the passion alive at BISD. There is no room for laziness, no time for contentment. Passion is the cornerstone of past accomplishments as well as the foundation of future achievements.

fueling the fire

In his comments, Anderson cites training as the way to fortify passion in his organization. He highlights an important point: critical as education can be in initiating passion, it can be even more valuable in sustaining it. Associates may be overflowing with enthusiasm, but they still need constant encouragement and guidance in developing and using it. To ensure continued commitment and performance, the organization must find ways to fuel the fires of passion. It must take measures to institutionalize it, to make it a permanent and integral part of its culture.

Southwest Airlines excels in this area. It has a Culture Committee, which is dedicated to protecting and promoting the organization's core passions. The committee is made up of associates from all areas of the business who exemplify the Southwest Spirit. Each associate serves for two years, volunteering time outside of the normal work schedule. During their tenure, associates engage in a wide variety of activities to communicate passion throughout the organization. Kevin and Jackie Freiberg use these words to describe the committee: "It is not a group of headquarters staff and managers who use their power to tell the rest of the organization how to behave. Rather, it is a group of shamans, spiritual teachers and organizational storytellers" (Freiberg and Freiberg, 1998, p. 166).

There is after all great power in history. If passion has been present from the beginning, then sustaining it entails steeping associates in the spirit and tradition of the organization. Gateway also has its raconteurs, who are responsible for communicating the passions that inspired its phenomenal growth. In an effort to capture this passion, the company's director of corporate culture recently produced a video titled "Gateway Spirit: What Was Special About Gateway." The video contains excerpts from interviews with some of the original Gateway employees, who are identified by their early badge numbers. For example, Badge #7 was the seventh employee, nothing to sneeze at considering the organization now employs thousands of people worldwide. What these employees communicate very clearly and powerfully is the spirit of experimentation, innovation, and commitment to customers that characterized Gateway in its early days.

The director explains his motivation for making the video in this way, "You don't just go from doing $100,000 worth of business your first year to doing $9 to 10 billion worth of business without extraordinary risk-taking, extraordinary innovation, and extraordinary inventiveness. We don't want to lose any of that. Instead of just presenting them as abstract concepts that any company could follow, we tie them to the history of the company itself. We use it to preserve that sense of passion and that sense of humanity." As part of his initiative to spread and sustain the organization's core passions, he has started showing the video to employees both new and old. After viewing it they can better appreciate the small-town, human ideals that their multinational, high-tech organization is trying to pursue.

One of the many ways McLeodUSA seeks to strengthen and communicate its core passions both inside and outside the organization is through its Passion Team. The team consists of approximately twenty employees who focus on finding ways for associates to have fun and become active in the community. They energize employees by organizing social events and volunteer efforts, constantly reminding them that passion is what fuels success at McLeodUSA and is in fact the reason for its existence.

Confronting Challenges

No matter how passionate the organization, it cannot control all the factors that determine its success. All will from time to time confront challenges that test the strength of their passion. PSS/World Medical is all too aware of this. The company had experienced exponential growth and had plans in place to hold an initial public offering in 1993. The election of Bill Clinton to the U.S. presidency in November 1992, however, presented challenges PSS never anticipated. Because the president and first lady were making a lot of noise about health care reform, the market became hostile to those involved in the business. The reaction was so severe, PSS not only had to call off its IPO, it also had to implement widespread pay cuts to prevent its bank from demanding immediate repayment of its loans. That was a challenge even for Patrick Kelly and his fun-loving, customer-crazy crew.

Kelly recognized the threat this downturn presented. He also understood that the business could survive it if it could preserve the passion that had fueled its success. He demonstrated his confidence and continued commitment by taking a 30 percent cut in pay. He then asked 525 associates to take cuts as well, the percentage depending on their position. Senior management accepted double-digit decreases while truck drivers were asked to forgo only 3 percent of their income. In a weaker organization, employees might have jumped ship, but not a single PSS employee left in the wake of the decreases. When the Clintons backed off a year later and the company successfully launched its IPO, all who had accepted cuts were rewarded with stock options.

PSS experienced another blow in 1999 when the Balanced Budget Act was passed. The company had just acquired Gulf South Medical, a nursing home supply company. The Act cut Medicare reimbursements to nursing homes and struck a potentially debilitating blow to the industry. The result for PSS was a plummet in its stock price and an uncertain future. Kelly admits this most recent challenge has been traumatic. The organization was forced to lay off a hundred employees and shut down some of its branches. He says, "It's been very hard to hold onto this passion when external things affect the company and there's nothing we can do about it. It's been a time when we have to communicate more than ever. People have to understand that even though there are things we can't control, there are other things we can. We can control taking care of customers. We can control having fun. We do those two things and everything else will fall in line."

These two things of course are the core passions of the organization. They are the forces that guide it through thick and thin. Kelly does not doubt that the circumstances that threaten his business today are only temporary. He firmly believes the tide will change and that as baby boomers enter their retirement years, the nursing care business will boom. And skeptics must remember that despite its current troubles, the organization Kelly and his associates have built is still generating over $2 billion per year in sales! By remaining focused on passion, PSS will weather the storm and emerge stronger for it. Associates' loyalty through past struggles indicates the passion they share and their willingness to make sacrifices in preserving it.

When facing challenges, organizations must look to their passion for sustenance. Though there may be a temptation to abandon it or give up on it, they must draw on it instead. It can provide a critical source of strength and consistency that transcends circumstance, that enables success when it seems impossible.

Accepting Change and Adapting Accordingly

PSS must accept the change that has swept its market. It cannot ignore it or pretend it has not happened. This holds true for all organizations whether the changes they face pose positive or negative consequences.

In Chapter Six I discussed the ways Clarke American has anticipated and accepted changes in its industry. Originally focusing on printed checks, it has now expanded its product and service offerings to include call center support for banks. This addition to the business was not a random attempt to compete, but a concerted move to increase the company's potential for growth and to provide value to its customers. Though many organizations spread into areas that do not reflect core passions, Clarke American's move into phone support was a natural extension of its passion for customer service based on its core competencies. Because the organization knows banking and knows its customers, it also knows how to provide the services they need. Because it is passionate about doing so, it can adapt to their changing needs and excel at the same time.

Gateway has done the same thing in expanding the range of services it provides. In seeking to be the customer's trusted guide to technology, it has broadened its horizons far beyond building personal computers. It is "moving beyond the box." Gateway now provides sales, support, and service to businesses and individuals and is making moves into the Internet. These changes have required the organization to move its headquarters from the small Midwestern town of its birth to what one executive jokingly called "Surf City." They have compelled it to grow from a handful of employees to thousands. They have prompted leaders to ditch the cow, but never the spots.

Through all the changes the bottom line remains the same, and is epitomized in the company's new slogan, "Keeping it personal. Making it simple." Gateway remains committed to its core passions and is working ardently to build bigger and better services around them. No matter how things change, it is clear that Gateway will continue to be a humanizing force in the world of technology and a trusted guide in understanding it. Passion will continue to guide the organization's actions and define its future, regardless of where its offices sit and regardless of what others do.

Such consistency through change is a necessary part of any organization's action plan. If leaders and associates stay focused on core passions, they will be better prepared to face changes and see the opportunities they provide for building them. If they waver in their commitment or lose sight of what drives them, then the choices they make could lead to decisions that are out of alignment with the organization's purpose—and more significantly that they will one day regret.

Recovering from Mistakes

Ben & Jerry's learned this lesson the hard way. Like all organizations it is not perfect. In raising the standard of social responsibility, leaders added an unusual internal challenge to their business. Making decisions based on both their social impact and the financial bottom line is a difficult process and added significant pressure to leadership. This commitment attracted the attention of critics and fans alike, and from the beginning the organization was subject to a level of scrutiny usually reserved for much larger companies.

As time passed, the core passions of producing great ice cream and giving back became blurred and the company got off track in its efforts. The stock price fell and the business world questioned whether it was possible for a socially responsible organization to also be profitable. Scrambling to raise revenues the company began pursuing more orthodox paths to profit. One leader describes the change as a shift from the free-spirited, loosely structured practices of the early days to the tightly controlled, rule-driven environment more typical of a large corporation.

This change in focus undermined morale and left associates dispirited. They were working harder than ever but still losing market share. That was the situation when the company brought in Perry Odak. He was an experienced turnaround artist and knew how to get the business back in line. More important, he was passionate about doing so without abandoning the social mission of the organization. He wanted not only to save the business but also to show it could achieve its higher goals at the same time.

One of the first things Odak did was examine how the company's core passions were being employed. There had to be a reason that its unique and excellent products were being overlooked in the marketplace. In his analysis, he was shocked to learn that the company had never used traditional forms of advertising. While it only relied on public relations to further its social objectives, it did little to educate consumers on its products. The PR had certainly been effective in one sense; public awareness of the company rivaled that of corporate giants such as AT&T. But while people recognized and respected the company, they did not necessarily know what it did. Only half of those who knew the name actually bought its products!

Obviously if Ben & Jerry's was going to stay profitable it had to sell its products. Odak suggested to leaders that it was time to start advertising. He met with some resistance, but eventually everyone realized there was no alternative. Executives worked together to outline a strategy that would create product awareness while remaining true to the organization's social mission. They learned that both could be accomplished simultaneously without betraying the organization's basic beliefs.

Since Odak came on board, Ben & Jerry's has regained its momentum and is once again growing in market share and profitability. The company still makes mistakes, but has learned to recognize them earlier and take steps to rectify them much more quickly. A case in point occurred when Ben & Jerry's moved into foreign markets without considering the social ramifications of its actions. As Odak explains, "There was no social mission; we were just selling product. So we pulled back and said, 'Wait a minute. We're not going to sell ice cream into these marketplaces, make profits, and bring them back to the United States. We need to return something to the communities we're selling in around the world. We need to stand for something good as part of us doing business in those communities.'"

Ben & Jerry's faces a unique situation because it is treading into territory few businesses its size have entered. Certainly the organization is learning as it goes. But as leaders learn to focus on core passions in sustainable ways, they will pave the way for the company to prosper in ways Ben and Jerry themselves might never have imagined. By recovering from their mistakes, making the necessary adjustments, and embracing passion in wiser ways, they reinforce the emotion that built Ben & Jerry's and ensure it holds fast to the forces that define it.

Seeking Opportunities to Build Passion

Keeping passion alive is not just a matter of defending it. It also involves seeking opportunities to expand it. This can involve making moves that more conservative organizations might view as dangerous or threatening. Before their merger EarthLink and MindSpring were heated rivals. Though both companies provided similar services and were passionate about serving customers, there were many differences between them. MindSpring had been founded as an exercise in business dynamics while EarthLink had always been first and foremost about the Internet.

In considering the merger, the question for leaders was whether these passions could coexist. Would one have to be pursued to the exclusion of the other, or could they actually work together to fulfill the objectives of both organizations? While many would have dismissed the possibility without much consideration, leaders were motivated by their strong desire to keep their organizations moving and growing. They understood that their passions were not static and that their survival did not preclude change.

Both MindSpring and EarthLink were tremendously successful in building their businesses. But in a field where most competitors their size were affiliated with much larger organizations such as Microsoft and AT&T, they had to be on the leading edge of both technology and service to remain competitive. Though both were growing rapidly on their own, leaders realized that together they could move even faster. By pooling their talent and resources, they could make even greater progress in developing their Internet strategies and technology. This would in turn enable them to provide a higher level of service to their valued customers.

Keeping an eye to passion, leaders waded through merger waters carefully. In negotiations, Charles Brewer and the MindSpring leaders emphasized that the company's Core Values and Beliefs must remain a guiding force in the new organization. EarthLink leaders agreed, but added a core v alue of their own to the list: "We love to compete, and believe that competition brings out the best in us." While MindSpring was certainly competitive, it had not focused on competition as a means to excellence the way its West Coast rival had.

There were many more details of the agreement, but the result was what leaders emphatically termed "a merger of equals." No one organization would prevail in terms of power or presiding passions. The new company would be called Earth-Link and its headquarters would be in Atlanta (at the Mind-Spring offices). It would maintain a fervent focus on customers and remain committed to Charles Brewer's passion for building a great organization and EarthLink's passion for the Internet.

Time will tell whether the merger is successful. It seems likely, given the level of passion both partners bring to the table. Joining forces represents a commitment by each to strengthening core passions and creating opportunities to explore them in new ways. Both admit they have much to learn from each other and are excited at the prospect of their future together.

MindSpring and EarthLink's decision to merge was an aggressive step for each in preserving passion. Each understood that having passion is not enough: to stay ahead organizations must use it, grow it, and keep it vital. By following the practices I have outlined in this chapter, maintaining passion over the long term becomes not only possible but also probable. These steps, taken in conjunction with the measures outlined in Chapters Seven and Eight will ensure that passion flows freely and is used effectively no matter what circumstances confront the organization.

What to Do When Passion Is Missing

If, despite best efforts, the organization finds that passion is not thriving (or even surviving), leaders need to determine what is impeding their progress. There are many possibilities for the organization's struggles, and the strategy for addressing them depends on their origin. Usually one of three steps is required.

Passion Review

The organization must constantly strive to keep passion alive. This involves the following practices:

- Fighting complacency
- Fueling the fire
- Confronting challenges
- Accepting change and adapting accordingly
- Recovering from mistakes
- Seeking opportunities to build passion

Modifying the Action Plan

Even if the organization has prepared to face challenges, they may prove overwhelming when they actually occur. If associates are excited but unprepared to deal with bumps in the road, the answer may be to modify the organization's action plan. There are many reasons the existing action plan may be inadequate. Perhaps leaders did not account for factors such as increasing complexity in their market or the presence of a new competitor. Perhaps the milestones they set were too ambitious, or the time designated for aligning associates insufficient. Maybe they did not do enough to eliminate practices that drain passion or to create policies that build it. Whatever the case, if leaders firmly believe that the core passions they identified are correct, then they must find ways to realign the organization around them.

When modifying the action plan, it is critical that leaders not become discouraged by their past efforts, but view them as a learning experience. Given an underlying passion, continued commitment, and ample opportunity, they will eventually reach their goals.

Heightening Commitment

Passion does not always ensure commitment. If it is new or untested, it may wane in the face of adversity. If things do not progress as quickly as associates had hoped or leaders had expected, there is a chance people may grow fickle and abandon passion just as quickly as they adopted it. It is a shame when this happens, because organizations become more firmly entrenched in the unproductive ways of their past and lose the tremendous opportunity passion provides.

In cases where passion is present but those who share it lack conviction or direction, the answer is a heightening of commitment. Of course, the ways of achieving this are not always obvious, since a lack of commitment is the problem to begin with. There are many things leaders can do, however, to intensify the organization's efforts and ensure passion survives. These may include increased initiatives to create excitement in both associates and customers. Appreciation and input from outside sources often can provide the extra boost those inside the organization need to stick with their objectives and move to a higher level of performance.

By constantly communicating the core passions and providing opportunities for them to grow, leaders can model the increased commitment they require from associates. Once they catch a glimpse of the potential for change and improvement passion provides, associates will gain the energy they need to stand behind the organization's action plan and take it to a passion-driven plane.

Reevaluating Passion

Sometimes we are just wrong. If everything is going well for the organization but it still lacks the fire and edge that passion bring, then maybe the core passions leaders have identified are really just competencies or interests. The same may be true if things are going poorly and no one can muster the energy to stand behind them. If there seems to be no galvanizing force behind the action plan or no enthusiasm behind the changes being made, then leaders must consider the possibility that they have made a mistake and begin the process of identifying core passions once again.

You may question how this could be. How could a group of leaders committed to improving the organization be completely wrong in their assessment of its potential? The answer is simple. They are human. Seeking to create a human organization fueled by human emotions is of necessity a human process. If passion has been lacking for an extended time or leaders have never really experienced it themselves, they make mistakes in identifying it. The wonderful thing about humans, however, is that though we are fallible, we can learn from our mistakes. With each effort they make, and with each step the organization takes, leaders will learn more about the organization. In so doing, they will also grow closer to defining the passions that have the potential to make it excel.

Moving Forward

Though the potential for negatives exists when following an organizational passion plan, the possibility of positive change is far greater. In this chapter I have focused on challenges to maintaining organizational passion, but the reality is that once a group has found its core passions, it will be strengthened and rejuvenated by them. Even in cases where passion is not managed optimally, it enables organizations to endure hardships and rebound from failures. More often it prevents both from occurring. The passion-driven organization gradually becomes self-reliant, finding ways to overcome obstacles and create its own successes. It need not look outside its own doors for validation, as it is bolstered by the forces that define it. By always heeding and nurturing these core passions, it carves a certain future in an uncertain world—one in which Profit is always visible and the journey is always fulfilling.

As you move forward in following your organizational or personal action plan, complete the worksheet at the end of this chapter to brainstorm ideas for keeping passion alive. Imagine possible challenges and think of ways you might respond to ensure passion survives.

PASSION PLAN WORKSHEET #7

Step Seven: Stay the Course   How

A. Ways to Keep the Organization's Passion Alive:	Identify ways to keep core passions alive as the organization continues to pursue them. It is important to not let any initial challenges or difficulties discourage associates from moving forward. Consider the following:

Identify ways to keep
core passions alive as the
organization continues to
pursue them. It is impor-
tant to not let any initial
challenges or difficulties
discourage associates from
moving forward. Consider
the following:

- What have we done to help make our passion special in the organization?
- Have we taken the time and effort necessary to keep our passion alive? If not, what do we need to do differently?
- Do we need to recommit to pursuing our passion?
- Who can help us maintain our enthusiasm for the organization's core passions?
- What needs to be done to prevent complacency?

Passion Plan Worksheet #7 (cont.)

B. **Possible Strategies for Facing Challenges:**

Develop strategies for handling challenges and impediments to the organization's plan. If leaders and associates find themselves questioning their ability to carry out the plan, consider the following:

- Do we need to modify the plan?
- Are we truly committed to pursuing the organization's passion? If not, do we need to heighten the organization's commitment?
- Are there signs that indicate that the organization needs to reevaluate its passion?

Passion Plan Worksheet #7 (cont.)

C. **Ways That the Organization Can Sustain and Renew Its Passion:**

Identify ways that the organization can sustain its passion, as well as continually renew its focus on it. To do so, consider incorporating the following as part of the organization's routine operating practice:

- Accept change and adapt accordingly
- Recover from mistakes
- Turn to others for support
- Reevaluate passions periodically
- Modify action plans as needed

Passionism...

"As the organization grows, existing passions may evolve and new passions may emerge based on its successes."

CHAPTER 10

Realizing Profit

Moving On to Bigger and Better Things

Out of every fruition of success, no matter what, comes forth something to make a new effort necessary.
—WALT WHITMAN

Men achieve a certain greatness unawares, when working to another aim.
—RALPH WALDO EMERSON

The organizations that use this book will do so because they want something more, something better. In each case more and better constitute the organization's specific idea of Profit. There are, however, two types of Profit: that which you seek and that which you find. The outcomes leaders define in beginning the organization's Passion Plan are the Profit they seek. The positive outcomes that result from following it are the Profit they find. Often the two are the same: the organization begins with a goal in mind and reaches it. Just as often, though, they differ: the organization looks for one thing but finds another.

The Profit leaders envision today will be the foundation from which they view a new or more complete Profit tomorrow. Profit after all is no more static than is passion. It is at once a concept and a reality, a motivation and an accomplishment. Think of it not as an end but rather as a beginning.

Profit Sought

Passion is especially relevant in a time when traditional definitions of success are changing. Financial returns are still important, but organizations today often judge themselves by much tougher criteria. The Profit they seek involves making contributions to society and individuals that transcend monetary gain. The types of Profit I have observed include the following:

Endurance and legacy. The success of *Built to Last* (Collins and Porras, 1994) is a testimony to the growing desire to create companies that endure. Organizations have become institutions that stand for much more than a product or service. They embody the virtues and practices that build communities and improve individuals. Though specialties and strategies may change to meet market conditions, organizations can create something more, a legacy to pass on to future generations. Some think this notion unrealistic, but it is gaining in popularity. Charles Brewer created MindSpring not just to experiment with his beliefs about how a business should be run or what it should stand for, but to make an organization that would illustrate those principles for decades to come.

When passion is enlisted, there is also a strong possibility that the Profit the organization finds will differ from the one it originally sought. This is true because passion can open doors. It can expand horizons and create opportunities where before there were none. Consider the example of Disney Institute. When Walt Disney started Disney he probably never imagined the wealth of possibilities that would result from the organization's pursuing its core passions so effectively. His sights were set on delighting and entertaining the public, but because the company was so successful at doing this, it found other organizations clamoring to share its secrets. It also found increased opportunities to influence its customers as a result of the trust and warmth it inspired in them. Subsequently Disney leaders created Disney Institute not just as a means of expanding their business but as a forum for spreading their passion and helping others to discover their own. Walt Disney would undoubtedly agree that the Institute provides an invaluable form of Profit to the organization, one that in many ways exceeds his original goal.

Ben Cohen and Jerry Greenfield have also discovered the ways in which passion can bring about unexpected Profit. When they started Ben & Jerry's, they wanted to make great ice cream, earn enough money to live on, and give back to the small town they called home. As their passion flourished and their business grew, however, they realized that they could do much, much more. Through their operations and influence, they could actually begin to change the way the world views business. The path they have forged has not always been smooth, but the Profit they have found is undeniable. The organization they have created is no simple ice cream company. It has set a new standard in the business world and continues to stretch the limits of conventional business wisdom.

The Profit Ben & Jerry's seeks today has certainly evolved from the one Ben and Jerry sought in the early days. The organization possesses the same passions, but has increased possibilities for pursuing them. This has proven true for Earth-Link as well. The organization's passion for the Internet has enabled it to be a leader in providing access, but also to explore ways to improve and develop the Internet. Founder Sky Dayton was so excited by the tremendous potential of the Internet to open channels of communication and change lives that he created a new company devoted to finding, funding, and developing great Internet ideas. EarthLink is an investor in the company, called eCompanies, and stands to benefit in many ways from its success.

In each of these cases, passion has led to an extension or enhancement of the organization's definition of Profit. There are also times when it can bring about a complete change in this definition. Sometimes organizations find that what they thought mattered doesn't. A technology company with a core passion for innovation may discover that benefiting society is more important than outpacing competitors. An upscale restaurant chain with a core passion for haute cuisine may realize that pleasing customers matters far more than receiving critical acclaim. Whatever the case, by opening up to passion organizations become empowered to discover the new and exciting and to revise their ideas of Profit.

The Passion Cycle

By now you probably understand that passion and Profit are closely linked. I hope it is obvious that passion is the single

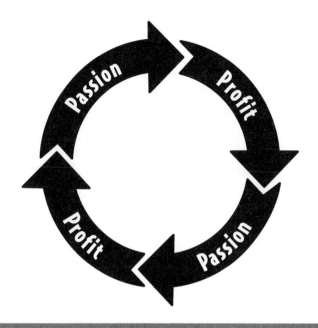

Figure 10.1. Passion Cycle.

most important factor in realizing Profit. I also hope you see that the process of following passion to Profit is not linear but a cycle that repeats itself time and again, as illustrated in Figure 10.1.

An organization can follow passion to one level of Profit and find its passions renewed and perhaps recreated. As conditions change and the organization grows, existing passions may evolve and new passions may emerge based on its successes. Leaders and associates may then be inspired to reach even higher levels of Profit than they originally envisioned.

Ultimately passion-driven organizations will be rewarded by their survival, a necessary form of Profit for any devoted to long-term success. In fact, it is my belief that as we enter a new millennium passion will determine those organizations that not only survive but thrive. Those that recognize passion will expand their potential by tapping into the organization's heart and unleashing their greatest force for progress. Those that don't will face increasingly daunting challenges and find it difficult to compete with the passion-driven competition.

Passioneering

If an organization remains steadfast in its commitment to its core passions, eventually this cycle will become second nature. The organization will no longer dwell on the individual steps; instead the steps will become a self-sustaining part of organizational performance. The organization will become self-actualizing, having a heightened knowledge of what it is, and what it can and should accomplish. It will build the future its past, current, and future leaders dream of by allowing what is best and most inspiring to be experienced in the workplace.

It is my hope as you take the message I have presented here into your organization—regardless of the position you hold—that it will be a force for change and progress, that it will plant the seeds of passion that will one day take root and transform the organization. As you embark on your mission, I wish you well and encourage you to let passion guide the way.

Profiled Organizations

For more information about the superior organizations profiled in this book, please visit the following Web sites.

Ben & Jerry's—http://www.benjerry.com

Brazosport Independent School District—
http://www.brazosport.isd.tenet.edu

Clarke American—http://www.clarkeamerican.com

Disney Institute—http://disney.go.com/Disney World/Disney Institute

EarthLink—http://www.earthlink.net

Gateway—http://www.gateway.com/index.shtml

GTE Directories—http://www.gte.com

McLeodUSA—http://www.mcleodusa.com

PSS/World Medical—http://www.pssd.com/wmi/index.htm

Southwest Airlines—http://www.southwest.com

Wainwright Industries—http://www.wainwrightindustries.com

References

Alsop, R. "Corporate Reputations Are Earned with Trust, Study Shows." *Wall Street Journal,* Sept. 23, 1999.

Amabile, T. M. *The Motivation for Creativity in Organizations.* Cambridge, Mass.: Harvard Business School Press, 1996.

"Apple and EarthLink Form Partnership to Deliver Best ISP Service to Macintosh Users." http://www.apple.com/hot news/articles/2000/01/earthlink

Bowen, E. *The Death of the Heart.* New York: Knopf, 1938.

Carlton, J. *Apple: The Inside Story of Intrigue, Egomania, and Business Blunders.* New York: HarperBusiness, 1997.

Chang, R. Y. *The Passion Plan: A Step-by-Step Guide to Discovering, Developing, and Living Your Passion.* San Francisco: Jossey-Bass, 1999.

Cohen, B., and Greenfield, J. *Ben & Jerry's Double-Dip.* New York: Simon & Schuster, 1997.

Csikszentmihalyi, M. *Flow: The Psychology of Optimal Experience.* New York: HarperCollins, 1991.

Csikszentmihalyi, M. *Finding Flow.* New York: Basic Books, 1997.

Collins, J., and Porras, J. *Built to Last: Successful Habits of Visionary Companies.* New York: HarperBusiness, 1994.

De Saint-Exupery, A. *The Little Prince.* New York: Harcourt, 2000.

Freiberg, K., and Freiberg, J. *Nuts: Southwest Airlines' Crazy Recipe for Business and Personal Success.* New York: Broadway Books, 1998.

Imperato, G. "Greetings from Idea City." *Fast Company,* Oct. 1997, pp. 140 ff.

"In Search of Leadership." *Business Week,* Nov. 15, 1999, p. 172.

James, W. *The Writings of William James.* (J. J. McDermott, ed.). Chicago: University of Chicago Press, 1977. (Originally published 1902.)

Kelly, P., with Case, J. *Faster Company: Building the World's Nuttiest, Turn-on-a-Dime, Home-Grown, Billion-Dollar Business.* New York: Wiley, 1998.

"Malcolm Baldrige National Quality Award: Ten Years of Business Excellence for America." Gaithersburg, Maryland: National Institute of Standards and Technology.

Maslow, A. *Toward a Psychology of Being.* (2nd ed.) Princeton, N.J.: Van Nostrand, 1968.

McLeod, C. E. *This Way Up: An Insider's Guide to the Climb of Your Life.* Cedar Rapids, Iowa: McLeodUSA, 2000.

"21st Century: Exemplary and Beyond." http://www.brazosport.isd. tenet.edu/pub/insight/AEIS.htm.

Index

H

Head-first organizations: core passions and, 66; head-driven approach and, 10

Health care reform, 222–223

Heart: awareness of emotion and, 54–58; Big Purpose and, 99–103; importance of starting from, 37; overcoming barriers to passion and, 58–60; Passion Plan Worksheet for, 62–63; returning to the, 54–61; starting from the, 37, 47–63; symptoms of lack of, 52–54, 62–63

Heart-first organizations, 48–50; core passions and, 66, 88; heart-driven approach and, 10–11

Heart of organizations, respect for, 10–11

High-tech industry, 130–131

Hiring: from within, 189–190; passion-centered, 158–160, 184, 185

History: discovering passions through, 84–85; sustaining passion through, 221–222

Holstein symbol and motif, 204–205

Humanitarian key profit area, 108–109

I

Ice cream, 95, 172, 205, 207

Ice cream containers, 128

Idea City, 160–161

Ideas: customer, 207; employee, 191–192

iMac series, 34

Immediacy, 61

Imperato, G., 160

Implementation, 147–181; aligning employees for, 156–160; assessment for, 152–153, 179; communication for, 151–152, 178–179; context and, 148–149; for employees, 176–177; investigation for, 149–151, 178; passion-drive policies and practices for, 164–165, 180–181; passion-inspiring physical environment for, 160–164, 180; passionate leadership for, 154–156; peak performance and, 167–171; performing in parallel for, 171–173; promoting a passionate outlook for, 165–167

"In Search of Leadership," 81

Inadequacy, feeling of, 53

Incentives, 192–194

Inconsistency, as symptom of passion deficit, 53

Indecision, 14–15

Unleash the Hidden Power of Passion

A wide range of Passion Plan products and programs by Richard Chang provides direction on how to integrate passion into all aspects of life and work, and improve personal, professional, and organizational performance, including:

The Passion Plan: A Step-by-Step Guide to Discovering, Developing, and Living Your Passion—Hardcover, softcover, e-book version, or book-on-tape (abridged audiotape or compact disc version)

The Passion Plan Workbook: An Application Guide to Discovering, Developing, and Living Your Passion—Softcover companion volume

The Passion Plan: Putting Your Passion to Work

- Videotape (with leader's guide)
- Workshop (half-, full-, or two-day session)
- Trainer Certification and ToolKIT™⁰

The Passion Plan at Work: Building a Passion-Driven Organization—Hardcover version

Keynote Presentations Based on *The Passion Plan* and *The Passion Plan at Work*

For more information or to order, visit

www.thepassionplan.com

or

www.richardchangassociates.com